We Are All Witnesses

We Are All Witnesses

*Toward Disruptive and
Creative Biblical Interpretation*

Mitzi J. Smith *and*
Michael Willett Newheart

CASCADE *Books* • Eugene, Oregon

WE ARE ALL WITNESSES
Toward Disruptive and Creative Biblical Interpretation

Cascade Books
An Imprint of Wipf and Stock Publishers
199 W. 8th Ave., Suite 3
Eugene, OR 97401

www.wipfandstock.com

PAPERBACK ISBN: 978-1-6667-1463-0
HARDCOVER ISBN: 978-1-6667-1464-7
EBOOK ISBN: 978-1-6667-1465-4

Cataloging-in-Publication data:

Names: Smith, Mitzi Jane, author. | Newheart, Michael Willett, author.

Title: We are all witnesses : toward disruptive and creative biblical interpretation / by Mitzi J. Smith and Micahel Willett Newheart.

Description: Eugene, OR : Cascade, 2023. | Includes bibliographical references.

Identifiers: ISBN 978-1-6667-1463-0 (paperback). | ISBN 978-1-6667-1464-7 (hardcover). | ISBN 978-1-6667-1465-4 (ebook).

Subjects: LCSH: Bible—Hermeneutics. | Bible. New Testament—Criticism, interpretation, etc.

Classification: BS2361.2 W4 2023 (print). | BS2361.2 (ebook).

Contents

Lists of Illustrations

By Michael Newheart

1

Prologue

*Testifying Texts and Witty
and Wayward Witnesses*

Mitzi Smith's Testimony about Testimony

TESTIFYIN' IS A SIGNIFICANT ritual in most Black church traditions. The Spirit of God moves and animates the individual to testify. *Testifyin'*, Geneva Smitherman, argues, is "a ritualized form of black communication in which the speaker gives verbal witness to the efficacy, truth, and power of some experience in which all blacks have shared. In the church, testifyin is engaged in on numerous symbolic occasions."[1] The normal time to tell and hear folks *testifyin'* in most Black Seventh-Day Adventist (SDA) churches is during Wednesday night prayer meeting. We also testified before and after baptism and communion services, at a designated pre-dawn hour during Black regional camp meetings, or at an annual watch night service. At the Fourth District Annual Conference of the African Methodist Episcopal Church (AME), ministers were sometimes asked to recite a Bible verse as a form of testimony when we answered annual roll call. Some participants scrambled for and through Bibles to find a text; others arrived prepared with a text in mind; and still others could spontaneously conjure an appropriate verse or favorite Scripture. Because I grew up in a household that encouraged me and my siblings to memorize Scripture, I had a soul-encouraging storeroom of texts from which to choose, depending

1. Smitherman, *Talkin and Testifyin*, 58.

on what was happening in my life and/or in the world around me. In the SDA Church, we committed to memorizing a verse a week, so that on the thirteenth Sabbath of each quarter, students from each class (from kindergarten to senior citizens) were expected to recite all thirteen Scriptures. As a teenager and young adult, I seldom disappointed my Sabbath School teacher, my mother, or myself. So annual roll call in the AME Church was a cakewalk.

In the Black church Scriptures are often invoked in the testimonies of the saints and sometimes Scripture constitutes the testimony; no other words are necessary. Testifying or bearing witness is an illocutionary speech act (an act of speaking that in itself effects or creates the intended action).[2] Sometimes the testimonies of Scripture or ancient human witnesses express the same hope, desperation, experiences, and challenges as modern readers. And often because we are taught to regard Scripture as *the Word of God*, as the sacred articulation of nothing new under the sun (Eccl 1:9b), we default to the human experiences, the language and testimonies in the biblical texts, even when our experiences and those in the Bible conflict. As a teenager, I remember hearing church folk testify by quoting the psalmist's testimony at Ps 37:25 as representative of or the same as their own experience: "I have been young and now am old, yet I have not seen the righteous forsaken or their children begging bread" (NRSVue).[3] Walter Brueggemann argues that the OT, including the Psalms, are testimony and countertestimony.[4] The psalmist's testimony troubled me, but, as a young person sheltered within the walls of my denomination, I did not give myself permission and lacked the critical interpretative tools to dissent.[5] It was not a testimony I shared with the psalmist.[6]

In church, my mother, Flora Smith, often began her testimony by reciting at least the first verse of Ps 23 in the King's English! "The Lord is my shepherd I shalt not want. He leadeth me beside the still waters . . . He anointeth my head with oil." Some church members stood to testify that "God is good!" Others were silent throughout the testimony service. My mother, like many poor Black religious folks, was just happy to see

---

2. Coady, *Testimony*, 25. See Austin, *How to Do Things*.

3. In our church it was quoted in the KJV.

4. See Brueggemann, *Theology of the Old Testament*; Brueggemann, *Living Countertestimony*.

5. See Bird, *Permission Granted*.

6. Smith, "Give Them What You Have."

another day, given the everyday challenges of life, and life in a racialized and gendered world! A few members shared special testimonies that made most folks who were struggling to survive to keep their heads above water from week-to-week envious and feeling spiritually deficient. I admit I often felt compelled to say something good. As the saints would say, if we don't testify, if we remain silent, "the rocks will cry out" (Luke 19:40; cf. Hab 2:11). Sometimes I yielded to the pressure. But I was most excited when I had something truly miraculous to share. It was not unusual for somebody to give a covetous-worthy testimony about how somebody paid their rent followed by how God is faithful if we are faithful with our tithes. The saints testified that God's faithfulness—the God who owned the cattle on a thousand hills (who needs cattle in the projects?)—depended a whole lot on our tithes! Such testimony was followed by a hearty symphony of "amens"; few dared remain silent or respond differently to such positive earth-shattering testimonies. *God is good all the time, and all the time God is good*, became a testimony staple. But that *ain't* everybody's testimony! In her commentary on Nahum, Valerie Bridgeman writes that Nahum "tempers his words by saying YHWH is 'good' or, as verse [3:]7a notes, 'Good is YHWH,' again leading with the attribute. Africana people who are recipients of certain kinds of Christianity will recognize the liturgical exclamation 'God is good [all the time] and all the time, God is good.' This confession sometimes allows people to deny suffering, pain, and apparent unjust responses from the Deity."[7] Testimony time is seldom for bringing your bad news, lament or complaints. Someone might quickly cut you off if you dared offer anything but an uplifting word, a Scripture, or praise to God, although saints with heavy souls will sometimes have their say. Hopefully the trend is different in some spaces and/or has changed during the COVID-19 pandemic.

Cain Hope Felder identifies testimonies (along with sermons, Negro spirituals, conversion narratives and call narratives) as "near-canonical sources in African American believing communities," and he queries "what is the relationship between them and the sacred [biblical] text?"[8] Felder responds that African American near-canonical sources like testimonies "contain information on African American self-understandings in an oppressive culture, they contain equally vital information on how we have viewed the sacred text as canon, wider sources as canon, and the canon

---

7. Bridgeman, "Nahum," 195.
8. Felder, *Stony the Road We Trod*, 54.

within the canon."[9] Further, Felder argues that we must examine the function and significance of testimonies, as near-canonical sources, for Black survival, maintenance of cultural identity and self-esteem within the context of oppression, the role of testimonies in the task of interpretation, and the relationship between near-canonical sources and the biblical text.[10] The testimonies of Africana peoples and those that make up the biblical text are contextual and contingent. They are sometimes disruptive of the silence that oppression and violence impose and other times they are oblivious to, complicit in, and/or supportive of oppression and violence.

Everybody's experience of testifying and testimony in the Black Church are not monolithic, not the same across generations, denominations, or congregations. Keri Day states the following about the process of testifying in the Black Pentecostal Church:

> Testifying about our stories of God's care involved telling the truth. We told the truth about hard matters. I remember people standing to testify about the social and economic predicaments they faced, telling the truth about the inequality of social structures and economic institutions. Others in the congregation would talk back, nodding their heads or offering high-pitched shouts to affirm that God would deliver the speaker (and themselves from the hardships of life. I also recall members who would stand and tell hard truths about the congregation—about fights, slights, and bickering among members—in hopes of illuminating the reality of broken community. Sometimes apologies were spoken in testimony service and people would find their way to the person who was wronged, only for screams and shouts to break out in celebration of restored relationships and healing from wounds. Testifying was about bearing witness to a God who could heal in the midst of brokenness and help us face the truth of who we were and could be, if only we could participate in the loving work of the Spirit.[11]

Testifyin in the Black community has never been confined to the church. Smitherman further asserts that "testifyin can be done whenever anybody feels the spirit—it don't have to be no special occasion. Like the Reverend C. L. Franklin, father of Aretha Franklin, might just get up in the pulpit any Sunday morning and testify to the goodness of God. Aretha talks about the greatness of her man and how he makes her feel in her

9. Felder, *Stony the Road We Trod*, 54.

10. Felder, *Stony the Road We Trod*, 54.

11. Day, *Notes of a Native Daughter*, 2.

well-known blues recording, Dr. FEELGOOD and that's testifyin too."[12] The boundless Spirit does not limit itself to the church, church folks, self-identified Christians, or a particular human constructed genre. Religious persons or Christians do not always agree on what constitutes inspiration or what is inspired; it is subjective. For example, sometimes self-identified Christians offer formal testimony in which they use the religious language of inspiration to refer to what we might arguably consider secular, the secular and sacred overlap. For example, on June 21, 2022, at the House Select Committee hearings investigating the January 6, 2021, attack on the US Capitol by a mob that attempted to disrupt the certification of the presidential election that elected President Joe Biden, Arizona House Speaker Rusty Bowers testified that former President Donald Trump pressured him to overturn the 2020 presidential election results. Bowers refused to do what Trump asked, saying that he regards the US Constitution as "inspired," which signals that Bowers believed that God's Spirit was active in the lives of the originators of the US Constitution and guided their work. Bowers may even regard the creation of the US Constitution as miraculous.

Some Black folks, who may not have been welcomed into or did not belong to Black churches, testified among and to the masses of poor oppressed Black peoples. Tupac Shakur testified about the world's hatred of Black women on welfare and encouraged Black women to "keep ya heads up."[13] When President Ronald Reagan labeled Black women as "welfare queens," middle-class people across race abandoned poor Black women on welfare, even though poor white women constitute the largest numbers of welfare recipients. In fact, many Black families were systemically disqualified from receiving welfare benefits.[14] Tupac testified in his rap music that "since the man can't make [a baby], he has no right to tell a woman when and where to create one . . ."[15] Tupac's testimony transcends race and is particularly poignant as the conservative US Supreme Court has effectively abolished *Roe v. Wade* (1973) in its decision in *Dobbs v. Jackson* (2022), overturning almost fifty years of precedence that had acknowledged women's rights to bodily autonomy and full humanity.

Bearing witness to the testimony offered in rap music, Lissa Skitolsky argues that "hip-hop culture has always served as an important source of

12. Smitherman, *Talkin and Testifyin*, 58.

13. Shakur, "Keep Ya Head Up."

14. See Hancock, *Politics of Disgust*; Zucchino, *Myth of the Welfare Queen*.

15. Shakur, "Keep Ya Head Up."

text and testimony about anti-black racism in the United States. . . . When underground rappers asked, 'Can I get a witness?' they were calling on their listeners to do more than simply enjoy their songs. Like the preacher, the rapper demands that his audience hears and responds to his testimony and aims to *agitate* and *stimulate* his audience to action"[16] (author's emphasis). Skitolsky testifies that "Rap music was born as a form of counter-testimony about the nature and source of the suffering of African Americans."[17] Hip-hop songs bear witness to the build-up of the prison industrial complex that disproportionately imprisons Black men and women in dehumanizing circumstances; they testify to the genocide of Black peoples in the United States from enslavement, criminalization, mass incarceration and other forms of oppression and systemic anti-black racism.[18] Growing up, I did not find Church testimonies typically politically disruptive in the way that rap music and hip culture has been.[19] Interestingly, a number of blues, soul, and rap music songs and albums bear the title *Can I Get a Witness?* indicating the centrality of the testimony or witnessing tradition among Black people in the US, in and beyond the church.

Folks (religious, spiritual or neither) with a testimony are eager to tell somebody. Testifying can be therapeutic for the person who testifies and a

---

16. Skitolsky, *Hip-Hop as Philosophical Text*, 4. Comparing rap music to rhetoric in the book of Revelation, Blount (*Can I Get a Witness?*, 100, 101–2, 103) argues that despite the cultural resistance and political orientation of rap music, one of the genre's "many problems, according to rap's numerous critics . . . [is a] refusal to balance an attentiveness to the gritty portrayal of the decimation of life in the inner city with a sense of transcendent, transformative hope. The result is a music form that elicits a feeling of ultimate hopelessness where the only way out is a path of social self-destruction." Blount also critiques the misogynistic worldview of rap, but the book of Revelation is just as guilty in this regard. Blount further argues that Revelation, like the spirituals "never gives up hope." I would argue the language of hope differs depending on context. I find the following words from Tupac Shakur's 'Keep Ya Head Up' a call to remain hopeful:

> And, un, I know they like to beat you [Black women receiving welfare] down a lot
> When you come around the block, brothers clown a lot
> But please don't cry, dry your eyes, and *never give up*
> Forgive, but don't forget, girl, *keep ya head up* [emphasis mine]

17. Skitolsky, *Hip-Hop as Philosophical Text*, 11.

18. Skitolsky, *Hip-Hop as Philosophical Text*, 58. Skitolsky asserts that "in their frequent use of the terms 'genocide' and 'holocaust,' rappers do not minimize the harm of genocide but instead co-opt the term from its context in our anti-black sensibility of genocide in order to testify to the infliction of genocidal violence against black communities in the American past and present" (78).

19. For examples of the prophetic witness of Black women's sermons and speeches from the eighteenth to the twentieth centuries, see Riggs, *Can I Get a Witness?*

source of encouragement for the person who hears! François Hartog writes "there is no testimony without one to whom it is told. To whom do we speak and why? . . . [In] the religious aspect of testimony," the religious shapes the witness.[20] Hartog asks "How have human communities encouraged, shaped and staged, dramatized, controlled and also prevented this presence and this always potentially disconcerting word?"[21]

My mother, Flora Smith, often shared her life testimonies with us at home. In my experience, testimony services in church don't always allow for long stories. I have witnessed a leader or elder cut folks off when they got too long-winded, which is ironic given the pressure for everybody to get up and "say something on behalf of God" or "praise God's name." But that something should be "short and sweet." "Everybody ought to have a testimony." After my mother had her first major stroke, I asked her to write some of her testimonies so that we would have them when she was no longer living. My favorite is about the time she stood at the bus stop with no bus fare and a bus ticket floated through air like an origami plane and landed at her feet. She picked it up and boarded the bus to work. My mother had a second similar experience, but too many times she had to walk to work in the freezing cold.

Testimony time in the Black church could encourage the discouraged, which could be viewed as political considering that anti-Black racism prefers that Black people remain discouraged, silent, passive, apathetic, invisible, and hopeless. Some folks would leave testimony service uplifted and able to face their tomorrow. Others might exit wondering when God would show up for them in the same way God had for the sister or brother who testified how good God is. James Cone asserted, "For most evangelicals, revelation was found in the inerrant Scriptures, and one need not look elsewhere. I knew in my gut that God's revelation was found among poor black people."[22]

---

20. Hartog, "Presence of the Witness," 3.

21. Hartog, "Presence of the Witness," 3.

22. Cone, *Said I Wasn't Gonna Tell*, 11. Cone testifies about how he arrived at a place where he trusted his own "black experience as a better source of knowledge about God and Jesus. The black religious experience was less ideologically tainted because blacks were powerless and could not impose their view of Jesus on anybody. But often blacks mistrusted their own experience, turned instead to whites for their values, using the same white portraits of Jesus in their homes and in the stained-glass windows of their churches," 17.

I, of course, had a few testimonies of my own. In 1979, I quit my first job as a legal secretary after a tenure of about two years. I discovered how blatantly racist my employer was and that he had been paying me at least $500 less per month than the average white legal secretary. I had assumed extra duties as he was training me to do real estate title searches at the courthouse. I had earned a degree in the field before I started at his firm, was efficient and could type over 200 words-per-minute at best. I completed paralegal training while in his employ. It would not be easy for me as a Black woman to find another legal secretary job, even with my skill level, in Columbus, Ohio. Not long after leaving his law firm, I was asked to chaperon some young people who wanted to sell the SDA *Ministry Magazine* in downtown Columbus to earn money to assist with college expenses. I prayed, trusted God, and went to help the young people, instead of spending another full day looking for a job. When I returned home that day, I received a call from Jim Risen, the manager of his uncle's law firm; they also happened to be Jewish. Jim and I had attended paralegal school together at Capital University; we weren't close, just cordial. He said he heard (don't know how) I was looking for a job and offered me a job at his uncle's firm making $500 a month more than I had been making at the firm I left. Further, Jim said that I didn't even need to interview for the job because he knew my work. That had never happened to me before and never has since. I considered it a miracle and a testimony I couldn't keep to myself; I had to tell somebody!

In this book, we attempt to model how to engage in critical justice-oriented disruptive interpretation that places the testimonies of the vulnerable of our world, and our own testimonies, in conversation with the testimonies in biblical texts. This necessary dialogical work we bear witness to is liberatory and freedom championing. We encourage the mutual work of conscientization, as named by Paulo Freire.[23] We hope this work will assist in demonstrating how we can center the plight of the oppressed and vulnerable among us, to focus on justice and the God who lives in front of the text or in our world, and compel us to act toward unmitigated freedom, justice, equity, and equality for all.

The Spirit inspires testimonies, but it is always our choice to act courageously to disrupt oppressive and marginalizing systems, structures, policies, practices, theologies, and interpretations. As Carolyn Sharp argues,

---

23. Freire, *Pedagogy of the Oppressed.*

"courageous readings of the biblical text" attend to the Other or othering.[24] Indeed, disruptive biblical interpretation is courageous given the possible consequences of rocking or upsetting the hermeneutical boat or troubling the biblical waters upon which the church too often rides or sails quietly, passively, and complicitly along on the waves of oppression. The question is, how and what shall we testify in our world and by our behaviors or actions?

Testimonies or testifying can be understood as storytelling or coming to voice that is constructive and disruptive, as well as subjective. Biblical texts are human constructed. They are both human and sacred. As William Coffin writes, "if we conclude that the Bible is a human product, we are by no means denying the reality of God. Rather, we are simply admitting that there is no escaping our personal and cultural history, nor the personal and cultural history of all writers, no matter what their subject matter."[25] God is not synonymous with the Bible. Further, as Walter Brueggemann argues, "the Bible requires and insists upon human interpretation that is inescapably subjective, necessarily provisional, and, as you are living witnesses, inevitably disputatious."[26] Yung Suk Kim writes that the meaning readers construct from engagement with texts is "always subjective; meaning does not inhere in texts."[27] Brian Blount asserts our humanity "signals contingency, limitation, context. Because they are human, our spirits always encounter God *through the context* in which God finds us and we find ourselves. This means that each one of us as individuals or in community *always* perceives God—and what it is that God wants from us—*differently*."[28] All testimony is subjective, regardless.

Biblical texts are not self-interpreting, they require readers/interpreters—no reader escapes her, his or their own dynamic subjectivity, including individual and collective traumas, cultural formations, theological commitments, formal education, and so forth. My formal critical training, as an interpreter of biblical texts, began when I was an MDiv student at Howard University School of Divinity (HUSD) in the mid-to late nineties. In fact, my co-author, Michael Newheart, was the first biblical scholar from whom I learned to interpret biblical texts while at HUSD. Truthfully, I intended that my first teacher would be Cain Hope Felder, but he was on study leave

---

24. Sharp, *Wrestling the Word*, xii, 37–42.

25. Brueggemann et al., *Struggling with Scripture*, 2.

26. Brueggemann et al., *Struggling with Scripture,* 13.

27. Kim, *Biblical Interpretation*, 29.

28. Brueggemann et al., *Struggling with Scripture*, 54.

in the fall of 1995. Thus, I enrolled in Dr. Newheart's courses Introduction to New Testament I (Gospels and Acts of the Apostles) in fall 1995 and Romans and Galatians in fall 1996. I was determined to learn how to do this thing called "exegesis." While I no longer use the term "exegesis" to describe how I interpret biblical texts, I value the skills I developed. The exegetical preaching courses that Drs. Gene Rice and Evans Crawford co-taught in Psalms and Kings were also quite formative. I am honored to write this book with Dr. Newheart. I find it difficult calling my former professors by their first names; I oscillated between Dr. Felder and Cain, and I alternate between Michael and Dr. Newheart. Our text is a metatext in that we testify or bear witness to sacred testimonies. Indeed, our testimonies, as human beings created in and to reflect God's image, are also sacred. Testify, Michael, testify!

Michael Newheart's Testimony about Testimony

My story begins in New Genesis Baptist Church (NGBC). Yes, that was the church I attended when I first came to Washington, DC to teach at HUSD in 1991. This small, predominantly African American church was meeting over the local hardware store just a couple of blocks from my apartment. I could sleep in and still make it to worship! The church was pastored by an African American woman who earned her DMin from HUSD, Rev. Dr. Diane Brenda Williams. The worship service in that church typically included a time for testimonies. This was an unstructured time in which anyone could rise and talk about how God had blessed their lives. I particularly remember the pastor's mother, Mrs. Williams, giving testimony to what God had done in her life. She was not a member or regular attendee at NGBC; rather, she was typically found at a larger church across town, Walker Memorial Baptist Church (WMBC), where she had raised her family. Nevertheless, she had special status at NGBC because she was the pastor's mother, and she was an influential member at WMBC. When she was at NGBC, Mrs. Williams would often testify, using much the same words as she had on previous visits.

I remember only two things about her testimony. First, I remember her presence much more than anything that she said. Mrs. Williams was a woman who was "well-acquainted with the Lord." She embodied a certain gravitas. Her children were pillars in the community, working in ministry, in academia, in law, and in real estate. Second, I remember that she always closed with these words: "Pray for me, and I'll pray for you." Mrs. Williams was a "praying woman." She knew the Lord and regularly spoke to him (and Mrs. Williams's God was a "him"). That gave her power in the congregation, and it lent power to her daughter, The Rev. Dr. Williams. If the pastor had a mother who was a praying woman, then the pastor must be a praying woman too.

Her testimony created community in that she invited others into her prayer. She exhorted people to intercede on her behalf, and she told them that she would intercede on their behalf. It was "Holy Triangulation," between God, Mrs. Williams, and us. Although she was a member of WMBC, she exercised power in NGBC through prayer, through praying and being prayed for. "Pray for me, and I'll pray for you," she always said with gusto, bobbing her head to the words, as if she was praying right then, as if she knew our needs before we asked. As we listened, we prayed for her, praying that she would pray for us, for that was her work. So, she testified.

We will argue that the Bible is a canonized collection of testimonies. The concept of testimonies or testifying is employed as a conceptual and guiding framework for thinking about biblical texts and interpretation. (We are thinking of testimonies in an ancient sense, John 5:39, and modern sense as in testimonies offered in faith and other communities as noted above). Testimony can be understood as storytelling that is constructive and disruptive, as well as subjective. Biblical texts, which we consider both human and divine, both sacred and secular, as well as methods of interpretation converge and diverge based on unique and overlapping approaches. This book privileges justice and creativity in its approach to biblical interpretation.

Primary in people's minds is testimony that one would give in a court of law, that is a formal testimony. We emphasize, however, the testimony that one offers in a Christian congregation, especially in the African American tradition, or even among persons who may identify as spiritual but do not participate in a Christian congregation, such as members of the Hip-hop community.

There are similarities and differences between formal testimony offered before a court or other formal hearings and those shared in religious services. Both involve personal experience. They both involve a narrative. Legal or formal testimonies involve "just the facts, ma'am," that is, only what the person has seen, heard, sensed. Church testimonies about physical healings or miracles involve interpretation but also evidence—not just

"I was healed," but "God healed me." Sometimes they involve supernatural means, and other times they occur by "natural means." In the former, the situation is so dire that there is no other help but God. No natural means can help. The problem is hopeless. The witness then does something: prays, attends church, reads their Bible, performs faithful actions, and so forth. Then, God responds (miraculously). In some cases, God works through natural means (people, medicine), nevertheless, the witness considers God as the source and to whom gratitude is due. *There is no external validation for the testimony.* The witness often says, "For God is my witness." Other stereotypical phrases are used: "But God. Only God." Sometimes Bible verses are quoted, which further interpret the witness's experience. The Bible becomes an additional witness to corroborate the witness's testimony.[29]

Testimonies are narratival, that is they are story-based. They have plot, character, and setting. The plot might be summarized as: God has worked a miracle in my life. The principal characters are God and the witness. Furthermore, they are also communal, and they have to do with power.

I have my own "fourfold" experience with testimony. First was the Lay Witness Mission (LWM). The name really kind of sums it all up: These were lay people (non-clergy) who would go to witness (i.e., give testimony) in a church different from their own. They were on a mission. My church, Second Baptist Church in Liberty, Missouri, hosted a LWM in April 1971. I did not attend the events on Friday and Saturday, but I did attend the closing Sunday morning service, in which many people came forward to rededicate their lives to Christ because they had been so moved by the testimonies of the weekend.

LWM came out of the United Methodist Church,[30] so I also participated in "Lay Renewal Weekends" (LRW), the Southern Baptist version of LWM.[31] LRW is the second phase, and the third phase occurred when I taught at HUSD, a historically black theological institution, and I began to experience "the Black church," specifically through the lens of one such Black Church in the 1990s, NGBC, where testimonies were often a regular part of worship services, as mentioned above.

Fourth and finally, I began participating in the Religious Society of Friends (Quakers) in the mid-nineties, and I heard much about Quaker testimonies (i.e., principles, tenets, guiding values), such as peace and

29. This approach is not different from that of the Gospel of John. See chapter 5.
30. Billman, "Revival Roots."
31. Noah, "Lay Renewal Weekends Lift Churches."

truth, sometimes summarized in terms of SPICES (simplicity, peace, integrity, community, equality, and sustainability).[32]

I would like to point you to a funny video entitled "How to Testify in the Black Church" by the comedy team The Playmakers.[33] This satirical video sets forward four principles of testifying: (1) Give honors; (2) repeat a popular phrase or Scripture; (3) blame the devil for everything; and (4) overexaggerate a story. If you have not viewed this video, please do so *now*.

It is striking how the four principles fit the Bible itself:

1. The Bible certainly gives honors. It gives honor to God first. The Bible begins, "In the beginning, God created . . ." (Gen 1:1) Two books in the Bible don't mention God at all (Esther and Song of Songs). Nevertheless, God is the central character, the one that makes it all right, that makes a covenant with a chosen people. The Bible is the book of God. It testifies to God's action in the world. Honors are also given to the ancestors: Abraham, Moses, David, Jesus. (These ancestors are typically male. The Bible mirrors and constructs a patriarchal world.)

2. The Bible repeats some lines. For example, Exod 34:6 often appears: "The Lord, a God merciful and gracious, slow to anger, and abounding in steadfast love and faithfulness" (see Num 14:18). In the prophetic literature, we often read the phrases "the Word of the Lord came to . . ." and "Thus says the Lord." For example, in Jer 16:1–3, the prophet says, "The word of the Lord came to me . . . For thus says the Lord . . ." This latter phrase appears twice in verses 5–9. We see this pattern throughout the Hebrew prophets.

3. Unlike the Playmakers, the Bible does not blame the devil for everything. The devil is a minor character in the Bible. The Bible does, however, attribute humanity's condition to supernatural forces, primary of which is God but also includes angels and demons. These powers hold humanity in thrall.

4. The Bible is certainly full of overexaggerated stories. A man calls himself Legion because he has thousands of demons that Jesus casts into thousands of swine (Mark 5:9–13). Jonah is swallowed by a gigantic fish, in which he resides or survives for three days and nights (Jonah 1:17). The Hebrews leave Egypt, pass through the Red (or Reed) Sea,

---

32. Connecticut Friends School, "S-P-I-C-E-S." See also Friends Community School, "Mission and Values."

33. E-News Now, "How to Testify."

and the waters on both sides of the sea are in a heap (Exod 14:22, 29). These are undoubtedly fantastic stories, which exaggerate life as we know it. Must these testimonies be true to be valuable and inspiring? Or is it most important that what they testify about the presence, power, and mercy of God is true?

How This Book Came To Be

Less fantastic is the story of how this book came to be. Smith was my student at HUSD in the mid to late 1990s. She refers to me as her "first biblical studies teacher," and indeed, there she was in my NT intro class on Tuesday nights in the fall of 1995, along with about twenty or thirty other students. I noted that Mitzi was quite quiet, but she really shone on her exegetical papers. Her paper on the stilling of the storm in Mark (or was it the walking on the water?) was exemplary, and I used it for several years as an example of an excellent paper.

Smith went from HUSD to Harvard, where she earned her PhD in NT studies. And from there she went to Ashland Theological Seminary, Detroit campus, and from there to Columbia Theological Seminary in Decatur, Georgia. I wrote letters in support of her tenure application at Ashland and her employment application at Columbia. And Smith would later write a letter in support of my tenure at HUSD. All were successful!

So, we have kept in touch. During a conversation over Messenger in August 2020, Mitzi said that she was interested in writing a book on biblical interpretation, and that she would like to have a co-author. I agreed to do so. Mitzi has been prolific; her writings have been exegetically stellar and passionate for social justice. It would be fun, I thought. And it has been!

How This Book Proceeds

Part I consists of three chapters, and chapter 1 is this Prologue. In chapter 2, "Context Is Everything" we testify about our contexts for reading biblical texts, as an African American woman biblical scholar and a white male biblical scholar. In chapter 3, "(New) Testament Texts as Testimony," we present our case for the Bible and more specifically the NT as a collection of testimonies. The NT consists of documents that are produced to "tell forth" the fruits of religious experience. People have experiences of God, Jesus, or the Spirit, and they tell forth those experiences in narratives, epistles, or an apocalypse. Some authors say to the readers or hearers, God has done this for me, and God will do the same for you. Or, look, what God has done in Jesus and among the people through Jesus.

In the first six chapters of this book, we walk readers through steps or processes for doing biblical interpretation using our diverse reading approaches to interpreting biblical texts contextually as testimony and that centers social justice. Readers will notice that our methods converge and diverge as we focus on justice. We explore two passages from the Gospels (of Luke and of John), one from the Acts of the Apostles, one from the undisputed Pauline letters (Philippians),[34] another from the Deutero-Pauline letters (Ephesians), and a pericope from the book of Revelation/the Apocalypse of John. Smith demonstrates how she analyzes passages from an overtly contextual womanist perspective that centers contemporary justice issues. In each chapter, we name aspects of our context and how they influenced our selection of a passage to interrogate/interpret. The justice issue that we choose as a framework or lens for reading the passage is directly connected with the context we name. We encourage students to do the same. Further, we raise many questions, practice close analytical reading of each passage *and* analyze each within its own literary context, consider relevant historical contexts for understanding each pericope, and, as the final step, we encourage dialogue with diverse commentators and other secondary literature that does not relinquish the reader's interpretative agency. Engagement with commentaries and secondary literature should not be the student's first stop, but the final dialogical step in the interpretive process. Each chapter in this section provides examples of resources to consult. Our purpose is not to provide extensive lists of books, but to suggest a few relevant and diverse significant monographs, essays, commentaries, and/or dictionaries. We hope this book offers students a guide and models for doing disruptive, creative, and justice-centered biblical interpretation that breathes new life into the process and that is pedagogically accessible.[35]

---

34. Scholars generally consider seven Pauline letters as undisputedly or unambiguously written by the apostle Paul. The seven are First Thessalonians, Galatians, First and Second Corinthians, Romans, Philippians, and Philemon. The six disputed or Deutero-Pauline letters are Second Thessalonians, Ephesians, Colossians, Titus, and First and Second Timothy.

35. See Parker (*If God Still Breathes*) who uses the metaphorical language of God-breath and breathing in her discussion of liberatory biblical interpretation unobstructed by breathtaking authoritarian claims of whiteness-centered biblical scholarship buttressed by doctrinal claims of inerrancy and infallibility.

In chapter 4, Smith leads readers through an analysis of the encounter between Jesus and a woman with a chronic illness that challenged her posture so that she could only stand, perhaps, at a ninety-degree angle (Luke 13:10–17). She begins by describing her womanist justice-centered reading approach and how her contextual testimony of being raised by a mother whose leg muscles constricted, inhibiting her ability to walk and without access to adequate health care, influenced her selection of that particular passage. Her justice context invokes particular and sometimes unique questions of the Scripture. In chapter 6, Smith turns her attention to the Acts of the Apostles and particularly the story of the encounter between the Ethiopian Eunuch and the evangelist Philip (8:26–40), which is based on her reading of that story in her book *Womanist Sass and Talk Back.*[36] Chapter 8, "The Precarious Nature of Citizenship for the Marginalized (Eph 2:11–22)" offers a model for reading the passage under consideration through the lens of the justice issue of the reality of citizenship for marginalized or oppressed groups within a racialized nation built on the genocide of native indigenous Americans and the enslavement of Black persons and where more than half the country insists upon white supremacists nationalism. Toni Morrison writes that the problem with "nationalism is not the desire to be master of your own house, but the conviction that only people like yourself deserve to be in the house,"[37] and as co-tenants and co-owners.

In chapters 5 and 9, Newheart examines documents in the Johannine literature, specifically the Gospel of John and the Revelation to John respectively.[38] The argument is not made that these documents are from the same author, nor that they arose out of the same community. The vocabulary, style, theology, and historical situation are much different from one another. The Gospel and Epistles of John are similar, however, probably arising out of the same community of believers, though not from the same pen. We will not deal with the Johannine epistles, though. We focuses on a scene from Jesus's trial before Pilate (John 18:33–38) and the introduction to the Revelation to John (1:1–8). In chapter 7, Newheart examines the so-called "kenotic hymn" (Phil 2:1–11). Newheart contends that in his letters Paul testifies to his experience in Christ. In chapter 10, the Epilogue, we

---

36. "Epistemologies, Pedagogies, and the Subordinated Other," in Smith, *Womanist Sass and Talk Back*, esp. 46–69. See also Smith, *Literary Construction of the Other*.

37. Morrison, *Source of Self-Regard*, 99.

38. His dissertation was published as Willett, *Wisdom Christology*. Also, Newheart, *Word and Soul*. When Michael E. Willett and Joyce O. Harman were married in 1993, they took the name Newheart from Ezek 36:26.

summarize our work and discuss what we hope readers will receive from our book.

We hope that after reading this book, you can testify that you have learned something helpful, and even transformative, about reading biblical literature and that you are a more enthusiastic and intelligent critical reader. Much peace to you as you read. We encourage you to keep a journal and write down your answers to some of the questions that we raise. And maybe you might even be inspired to draw or write poetry. No doubt critical and uncritical readings of biblical literature have been oppressive or supportive of oppression, including patriarchalism, sexism, tribalism, racism, poverty, rape, genocide, enslavement, queerphobia, and other forms of violence. But the opposite is and can be true. The deconstruction of oppressive texts brings relief to subjugated and violated readers and constitutes good news. Critical justice-centered biblical interpretation has certainly stimulated creativity, transformation, justice, and activism throughout the centuries. May it be so for you too! We are all witnesses! Asé!

Since this is disruptive *and* creative interpretation, we offer these poems:

We R All Witnesses
by Michael Newheart

We R All Witnesses
All, all, all. Yes, all. All, every one of us.
Witnesses. Wits. (And I'm only half right.)
Witnesses. Acts 1:8
You will be my witnesses: Jerusalem, Judea, Samaria, Galilee, and the
    uttermost parts
The udder-most parts (*Moooooooo!*)
Of the earth, which is dearth of mirth and spirth and lurth and I'm
    just making up words here.
We are *All* witnesses. All.
Witnesses to the peace, the joy, the love,
The Word.
All. We are all martyrs. To the cause of life.
We're dying. Dying. Shot. By active (not passive or even middle voice)
    shooters.

I am not a rooter of a shooter. I would rather ride my scooter.
All Witnesses. All *All*!
All!

A Plea to Readers of Sacred Texts!
by Mitzi J. Smith

Everything, everyone, everywhere is burning up
North in the suburbs, in rural areas, and urban cities
Global municipalities and hoods across ponds and at home
In motherlands and diasporas
Citizens across social class, race, ethnicity, gender, sexuality
Clash, suffer, and/or die in waves of heat
While namby-pamby heads stuck in smokey clouds
Looking no further than the mirrors on their walls
Cannot imagine fighting for a more just world
One that requires a revolution
Except the kind televised on the Capitol's steps
A return to a violent, bloody, and bleached past
Of bygone days resurrected by fists, guns, and that ole time slave
    religion—
Mired in patriarchy, genocide, enslavement, rape, murder, poverty
Of ancient sacred texts interpreted and bartered for land and
    submission
A sacred offering to folks with backs against crumbling walls
But who is the real sacrificial lamb in these testaments
About slaveholder religion and oppressive warring kingdoms—
Theocratic and theocentric monarchies, nation-states, empires,
    democracies?
Of Egypt, Babylon, Persia, Israel, Judah, Rome, Great Britain, USA—
Exposed and disrupted by colonial, postcolonial, and neocolonial
    testimonies
But the waking giant of white supremacy nationalism seethes and
    rages
No longer in the shadows but seated in our Courts and in the House
Its wrath gushes, like blood from an old ruptured wound, before our
    January Sixth eyes

Please! observe, lament, and testify to the signs of these times
No time to avert and shift our gaze, to look away
See and Testify! *about* the fugitive among us
Where is justice?
She is in flight from Mother Earth, scorching hot momma,
Lamenting unrelenting surges of racism and fury unleashed
Released on Black, Brown and impoverished folks, too often with
    impunity
On school children and folks at malls, night clubs, parades, in
    churches, temples, mosques
Punishing trans, transient, and exiled bodies
Fleeing hatred and the violence of poverty
Fugitives too tracking and tracing the scent of Mother Justice
In whose absence, human-made destitution flourishes
Sanctioned by human-birthed
Idols that graciously testify how "we are not like them "
They are but impoverished, impotent witnesses
To a God-inspired destructive and annihilating gospel that sanctions
Suppression and denial of rights for queer folks
Neighbors denied the right to marry whomever they love
Representatives of the state Loving vs. power
Mo' money loved while the
project of democracy remains unfinished
Black masses trapped in a school to prison pipeline
Or evicted from their homes
Children channeled into human- and sex-trafficking
Pregnant nine-year-old-raped-girls and boys and women
Transported across state lines
Boundaries mercilessly carved into pregnant female bodies
Everybody!
We cannot read as we've always read, ignoring the signs in our times
The Abuse of Momma Earth and her vulnerable children,
Let us not turn one more page to apologize
for the violence and hatred in our sacred texts and
Let us stop tip-toeing around the brutality
as if God is the vulnerable infant we must protect
God needs no defense except from theologies
That render God impotent in the world where the church resides

Too powerless to bring back the fugitive
The signs do not govern the times; we, with God, do!
Do read, re-read and do differently
Not as we've always read *and* been read
As if Goddess is an idol
Sculpted in the figure of a sacred tome
A hermeneutical tomb
Where justice is encased and
Where the cries of the oppressed are muffled
While evil thrives loudly
Let it prosper no more
Let the living read with signs of our times
Read against, above, and below the grain
Where God lives among us and beyond US
Calling us to expose, name, and challenge injustice and inequality,
   boldly
Summoning us, all of us, to testify and lament
And to entice the fugitive home
Grant her unmitigated citizenship
Protect Her rights
Promise Her loyalty and unwavering dissent
Our opposition to Her enemies
To injustice in all its disguises and habitats
In the pages of the sacred text, in our institutions, nation, and world.

2

Context Is Everything

Evil is understood, justifiably to be pervasive, but it has somehow lost its awe-fullness. It does not frighten us. It is merely entertainment. Why are we not so frightened by its possibilities that we turn in panic toward good?

—TONI MORRISON, *THE SOURCE OF SELF-REGARD*, 251

The Importance of Context

Context Is Everything.

Context Is Everything.

Context Is Everything.

WE SAY THIS SENTENCE three times because the idea is foundational. Another way to say the same thing—using one less word—is that context matters. It matters to me; it matters to you; it matters to all God's children, whether they realize it or not. Readers, situations, events, and texts have contexts. What is context? Context is simply that which accompanies a text in both time and space. A saying that has been bandied around a lot these days goes: "A text without context is a pretext."[1] A text always comes with a context. In the case of verbal texts, we might ask these questions: Who said

---

1. See https://www.fallacyfiles.org/quotcont.html#Note2, where the aphorism is attributed to Jesse Jackson, who himself attributes it to Donald A. Carson, who attributes it to his father, a Canadian pastor. Carson's version of the saying is "A text without a context is a pretext for a proof text."

it? Why did they say it? To whom did they say it? Where did they say it? When did they say it? What else did they say?

Merriam-Webster's online dictionary defines context as "the parts of a discourse that surround a word or passage and can throw light on its meaning" and as "the interrelated conditions in which something exists or occurs," as in its environment and setting.[2] Context is background and foreground or all within a text's sphere that helps to understand it. Context reminds us that nothing happens in a vacuum, that readers, situations, events, and texts are connected to and impacted by what surrounds them and contributes to their existence, formation, and meaning. Context contributes to understanding, and the absence of context to misunderstanding. Context provides perspective on the position, function and meaning of a text within a narrative, story, or other types of literature such as letters. How does a text contribute to the sequence of events within a narrative, story, poetry, or letter? Context reveals what precedes and follows an event, situation, narrative, poetry, letter or selected passage and how what precedes and follows is related to, clarifies, or fills knowledge gaps about the event, situation, narrative, story, poetry, letter, or selected text. The questions we bring to a reading of biblical texts arise from and can be driven by context—the reader's personal context, the context of the world in which we live, and the literary and historical contexts of the biblical text we seek to interpret.

Interpretation is achieved when readers critically engage the biblical text. As Yung Suk Kim asserts, "It is the reader who ultimately constructs meaning" each time they engage in the task of reading.[3] Thus, the reader's context in the world and how the world continues to shape or impact the reader and their context significantly informs and impacts what texts they choose to interpret and how they interpret. A reader's context consists of the experiences, expectations, history, places, cultures, people, traditions, circumstances, communities, ideologies, and so on that impact, inform, and/or shape them and vice versa. We may interpret one passage one way today and another way tomorrow because we have new and diverse experiences within a twenty-four-hour period that can shift our perspective, our concerns, our worldview, and our questions. In this chapter, we testify, beginning with Newheart's testimony, about our personal contexts as readers, our theological trajectories, our hermeneutical journeys. We also testify to

2. https://www.merriam-webster.com/dictionary/context.

3. Kim, *Biblical Interpretation*, 23.

how context has impacted and continues to impact how we read biblical texts. Our reading perspectives have evolved and continue to change. Some things remain the same, but we all experience change, especially if we are open to it. We will also provide brief examples of what it means to read biblical texts in their historical and literary contexts.

Michael Newheart's Testimony in Context about Context

Context is everything. I once told a class that I was going to have *Context Is Everything* inscribed on my tombstone. The next week a student came in saying that he remembered "Context is everything" because I said that I was going to have it on my tombstone. I had forgotten that I had said this, but I'm glad that it made an impression on him. I was telling my elder daughter Anastasia this story, and she said, "What do you mean 'tombstone'? I thought that you were going to be cremated." I said, "Oh yeah, I'm going to have 'Context is everything' inscribed on my urn." Anastasia simply rolled her eyes. (My daughters get a lot of practice in eye-rolling.)

I recently came upon a document that I had written nearly fifty years ago. It came without context. No date or other description appeared at the top of the paper. I think that it is quite instructive, so I will print it here in its entirety—unedited—and then comment on it.

Conversion Testimony

I accepted Jesus Christ as Savior on September 16, 1967, at age eleven during a Billy Graham Crusade. I subsequently joined Second Baptist Church, Liberty, Missouri and was baptized. My growth was steady until I entered junior high where I was more concerned about my popularity among peers than my relationship to God. This attitude continued into my first year of high school as I considered myself an intellectual, reducing God to secondary importance.

During this time my father became very ill and I did not understand why. While I felt spiritually bankrupt in this crisis, I was impressed with the newly found love and joy of my friends who had been involved in the Lay Witness Mission at my church. During one of the sharing groups I was so moved that I decided later to give God control of my life.

I began to meet regularly with the group, growing rapidly as God began to build love and understanding into my life. I was given the opportunity to go on Lay Witness Missions. My father died in October 1971, and God supplied many friends and relatives for comfort for my mother and myself.

In addition to Lay Witness Missions and sharing groups, I also grew through leadership opportunities in my church—planning and leading youth activities and speaking before groups.

The Lord is leading me now into the ministry as I was licensed in November 1975. Speaking through the leadership positions in church and through the Student Conference at Glorieta, New Mexico in 1974, God revealed that he was preparing this path for me. My position as teacher of the Bible study program at a summer youth camp served to reassure me of this call while teaching me a great deal about youth leadership.

Currently the Lord continues to teach me new things about Him, myself, and circumstances. He does this in many ways, such as Bible study, sharing with fellow Christians, and through the Holy Spirit leading in my life. Through this and much more, I find that God is making me a better person each day, equipping me so that I can aid others in their daily walk.

Exegesis of Conversion Testimony

Now I will exegete, that is, interpret, my conversion testimony.

I accepted Jesus Christ as Savior. That language sounds very much like twentieth-century evangelical language. One "accepts" Jesus as Savior. Sometimes it is "Jesus as Lord and Savior," or "Jesus as personal Savior." That is not biblical language, though. In the New Testament, one "believes in," "receives," or "confesses" Jesus (John 1:12; 3:16 et al; Rom 10:9, 10). *On September 16, 1967, at age eleven during a Billy Graham Crusade.* The crusade was held at Municipal Stadium in Kansas City, Missouri, where the Kansas City Chiefs and Royals played their home games. It was certainly characteristic of Graham for him to conduct his crusades in sports stadiums. I grew up in Liberty, Missouri, a suburb of Kansas City. As I often say, "I was born in Independence and raised at Liberty, so freedom is important to me!" I was born in Independence because Liberty at that time did not have a hospital. A whole slew of us, then, were born at the "Independence Sanitarium." *I subsequently joined Second Baptist Church* [2BC], *Liberty, Missouri and was baptized.* I had attended 2BC all my life. I went to the crusade on a 2BC bus. I intended to "go forward," which I did. Graham always said, "The buses will wait!" I can testify that that night they did!

My growth was steady—my spiritual growth that is, though I am sure that my physical growth was too—*until I entered junior high where I was more concerned about my popularity among peers than my relationship to God. This attitude continued into my first year of high school as I considered myself an intellectual, reducing God to secondary importance.* I still consider myself an intellectual, but I hope that I do not "reduce God to secondary importance." But it's interesting to note that I considered myself "an intellectual," which I thought would make me popular with my peers. Did it? I'm not sure. One is never sure whether one is popular or not, except of course if you're a politician.

During this time my father became very ill, and I did not understand why. This statement is indicative of the fact that I saw myself as an intellectual. I was trying to understand why in cosmic terms. My father had a severe case of diabetes, which led to all kinds of health issues (e.g., uremic poisoning). I do not say here that I was sad, or grieving, though I certainly was. Indeed, my relationship with my father was complicated. (Aren't all parental relationships?) In many ways, I was glad that he was ill because I did not have to experience his stern discipline. *While I felt spiritually bankrupt in this crisis, . . .* Wow! "Spiritually bankrupt," huh? If I understood why my father was sick, perhaps I would have felt spiritually "solvent." "Spiritually bankrupt," though, is strong language for a teenage boy to describe the state of his soul. I always have been given to hyperbole. ["I've told you a million times not to exaggerate!"] But with this extreme language was I intimating that my father was more important to me than I initially let on? A teenager needs a healthy role model and parent. How can one rebel against someone who is bedridden? His illness called into question my own health and masculinity.

I was impressed with the newly found love and joy of my friends who had been involved in the Lay Witness Mission (LWM) at my church.[4] LWM events at local churches centered on the out-of-town visitors sharing their

4. LWM grew out of the United Methodist Church, but they quickly became ecumenical. Southern Baptists developed their own such event, Lay Renewal Weekends. The concept is basically the same: A team of Christian laypeople (i.e., non-clergy) visits a church for a weekend Friday evening through Sunday noon. Events are held for the entire family, and each age grouping has their own schedule: adults, youth, and children. Depending upon the size of the youth group, we would sometimes divide the group into junior and senior high groups.

testimony, that is, the story of their conversion (or "rededication") to evangelical Christianity, in large and small groups. These testimonies could be quite dramatic, as witnesses told of their experiences of being lost or of being a "carnal (fleshly) Christian." Many of the participants were lifelong Christians, but they went through a time in which they did not feel "close to Jesus," which could mean several things, from not attending Sunday school and church regularly to experimenting with drugs and alcohol. I did not hear too much about sexual transgressions, though occasionally young men would talk generally about "sleeping around." (Confession: I always wanted more details!)

During one of the sharing groups, a Wednesday night youth prayer meeting, *I was so moved* by the effervescence of my friends *that I decided later to give God control of my life.* Again, this sounds very much like twentieth-century evangelical language. I am not so sure that God wants control of my life. I think that God wants me to be in control of my life with promptings from the Spirit and in the context of Christian community. Community is important for Christians of all ages, but especially for youth. I think that I was committing to the church's youth program and to this sense of meaning, purpose, and values that my friends had. It certainly spoke to the "spiritual bankrupt" condition of my soul. And many of the youth meetings were called "Bible study." For an intellectual such as myself, how cool was that, to discuss with others ancient, yet always contemporary, wisdom?

I began to meet regularly—Sundays, Wednesday nights, some Saturday afternoons and evenings, and daily prayer sessions—with the group, growing rapidly as God began to build into my life love and understanding Wow! I was busy, but it kept me off the streets—and away from home, where a sick father and an anxious mother resided.[5] Both the form and the content of this sentence is interesting. I "grew rapidly," as evidenced by greater love and understanding, which God "built into my life." My father was an amateur carpenter, so perhaps I thought of both Jesus and God doing the same thing. For whom did I have a greater love? And of what did I have greater understanding? Did I love my parents more? Perhaps, though all these youth activities took me away from them. Did I love my friends

5. Sunday school, Sunday morning worship, youth choir, Sunday evening worship, BSC (Brothers and Sisters in Christ, which were Sunday evening fellowship times at the youth minister's home), Wednesday night youth prayer meeting, occasional Saturday afternoon or evening activities, and even a brief daily prayer group that we developed at school.

more? I certainly felt more strongly toward them as we met together often. Did I love more those in need? Not particularly, *this newfound faith had very much an inward focus*. I do not remember us having service projects, although the pastor was involved in jail ministry. *I was given the opportunity to go on Lay Witness Missions*. I mention LWM three times in this brief document. They were obviously important to me. Witnessing is of supreme importance for evangelicals. "The fruit of a Christian is another Christian," we used to say. So, I was involved in the activity of witnessing. This was how God built into my life love and understanding: by sending me on LWMs. The focus in LWMs, however, was not on witnessing to "the lost," that is, to non-Christians, but to the "saved," or "sort-of-saved," that is, Christians who were not attending church activities, "lukewarm Christians," as we used to say, alluding to the Christians of Laodicea, Rev 3:16.

From my description of youth group, one might get the impression that 2BC was a soul-winning fundamentalist church, but nothing could be further from "the truth"! (A lot of people have said over the years that 2BC was far away from "The Truth.") Among Southern Baptist churches, 2BC was considered moderate to liberal, mainly because so many local college professors and staff attended the church. Little of that perspective filtered to the youth group, however, at least during my high school years.

My father died in October 1971, and God supplied many friends and relatives for comfort for my mother and myself. I was concerned about the state of my father's soul. He was not a Christian, or at least he did not participate in church activities. My father's people were affiliated with the Church of Christ (non-instrumental, i.e., they did not use musical instruments in their worship services, as opposed to the United Church of Christ, which is often considered the most liberal denomination), but my father was not a member or attender. He did not talk about religious matters. When I became interested in church youth activities, the only question he asked was "Are there good-looking girls there?" I said, "There are a lot of nice people there." Alas, I said nothing about the importance of my faith. I was afraid that he would reject me. I suppose that I was not a good witness.

In addition to Lay Witness Missions and sharing groups, I also grew through leadership opportunities in my church—planning and leading youth activities and speaking before groups. The Lord is leading me now into the ministry. This testimony might be classified as a "call narrative," for my focus is not on my conversion but on my call to ministry. *I was licensed in November 1975.* I was ordained in August 1980 at 2BC. *Speaking through the leadership positions in church and through the Student Conference at Glorieta, New Mexico in 1974,[6] God revealed that he was preparing this path for me. My position as teacher of the Bible study program at a summer youth camp served to reassure me of this call while teaching me much about youth leadership.* One might say that God spoke, and I spoke. God was leading me to lead.

Currently the Lord continues to teach me new things about him, myself, and circumstances (the world around me); the new things I have learned impact how I read Scripture. The "new things" become part of the context. *He does this in many ways, such as Bible study, sharing with fellow Christians, and through the Holy Spirit leading in my life. Through this and much more, I find that God is making me a better person each day, equipping me so that I can aid others in their daily walk.*

If I wrote the above narrative in the mid-seventies, I will sum up the remaining forty-plus years of my life briefly. After earning a BA at William Jewell College (WJC) as a psychology and religion major, I went on to The Southern Baptist Theological Seminary (SBTS) in Louisville, Kentucky to earn an MDiv and a PhD. Many of us who were at SBTS in the late seventies and early eighties wax nostalgic about it because the school has taken a decided theological turn in the last thirty years.[7] There I imbibed biblical criticism, peacemaking, and meditation.

Alas, I also imbibed white male supremacy. SBTS was founded by slaveholders.[8] During my MDiv days, I lived in Manly Hall. I was a Manly Man! The dorm was named for founder Basil Manly Jr. His father Basil Manly Sr. held forty slaves and was an ardent supporter of slavery.[9] But I have not revealed my personal connections to slavery. My maternal grandfather was Jesse Franklin Hall, who was named after his uncles, Jesse

6. I attended this conference three times during my college days. It was a highlight to gather with college students from all over the country. The date indicates that I was writing after August 1974, the date of the first Glorieta conference. I believe that I attended the next year. If so, then the paper was probably written the 1974–75 school year, which would have been my first year in college. The following sentence talks about my service as a Bible study teacher at a camp. I do not remember, nor do I have any documentation about when that summer camp was. In summer 1976 I became minister of youth at a KCMO church, so the camp must have taken place the summer of 1975.

7. See https://archives.sbts.edu/the-history-of-the-sbts/our-story/resurgence-1993-present/. This article speaks of the "conservative resurgence." Others would speak of the "fundamentalist takeover." See James and Leazer, *Fundamentalist Takeover.*

8. Banks, "Report Ties Southern Seminary Founders."

9. Allen, "Mohler Won't Remove."

and Frank James. Yes, *that* Jesse and Frank James, the outlaws from Clay County, Missouri—the county in which I grew up—who continued to fight the civil war long after it had ended.[10] So yes, I am the great-great nephew of Jesse and Frank James.[11] Their half-sister was Fanny Quantrill Samuel,[12] who married Joseph Hall, and they had Jesse Franklin Hall, who married Allene Groom and had fourteen children, among them Eleanor Ann Hall, who married Edward Efton Willett and had one son—me, Michael Edward Willett.[13] Jesse's and Frank's father Robert Sallee James was a Baptist minister, slaveholder, and one of the founders of my alma mater WJC.[14]

I said that I imbibed white *male* supremacy. During my two degrees at SBTS, I did not have a female professor, and at WJC there were no women on the religion faculty, neither in my time as a student nor my brief time as a professor. It's interesting that even though I considered myself "progressive" in both places, I did not give much thought to the whiteness or maleness of my two institutions. At neither WJC nor SBTS was there any sustained conversation among faculty or students about how white and how male the education was. The seminal text by Elisabeth Schüssler Fiorenza, *In Memory of Her: A Feminist Reconstruction of Christian Origins,* was published in 1983, when I was working on my doctoral dissertation, and none of my professors seemed interested in it.[15]

To pick up the narrative, I returned to my alma mater WJC to teach, and it was there that I heard God's call to overseas ministry. I had been a summer missionary to the Philippines in 1978 between college and seminary. I was in the southernmost island of Mindanao leading drama and puppet seminars. This was my first experience of being out of the country, and it transformed me. I was never the same. I remember clearly being in a hut sitting on a chair on the dirt floor. The woman held her baby as she served me. My eyes brimmed with tears. I did not know why. I only knew

10. See Stiles, *Jesse James.*

11. It makes for interesting conversation in churches during stewardship time!

12. Frank James (and perhaps Jesse) rode with William Quantrill, a Confederate guerrilla leader active in Missouri and Kansas known for his brutality. Frank's and Jesse's mother had remarried after the death of her first husband Rev. James. Her second husband was Dr. Reuben Samuel.

13. I took the name Newheart when my wife Joy and I married. Our theme verse was Ezek 36:26.

14. Historic Missourians.org, "Robert Sallee James."

15. I thank my good friend and colleague Tina Pippin for introducing me to the book. Otherwise, I'm not sure that I would have been aware of it.

that I was deeply moved by the poverty of the people and my relative affluence. I don't want to romanticize and objectify the people I saw. I also remember going to see the Blaan people in a remote village. I was told that I was the first white man that they had ever seen. I performed puppet shows for them, and my companion translated for me. I had seen the connection between the gospel and the poor. I had read of a Savior, who had said, "Blessed are you who are poor" (Luke 6:20). So, God called me to be on the side of the poor, and the best way for me to do that was to go to a majority world country and teach in the seminary. My gospel testified to freedom and liberation. Unfortunately, I was to find that the context in which I was to proclaim that gospel did *not* testify to freedom and liberation. Alas!

Before I headed to Venezuela to teach, I studied for a year of language school in Costa Rica. I became friends with a fellow Southern Baptist missionary who was much more conservative than I was. One night I visited him at his house to discuss theology. I left feeling invigorated and refreshed because I thought that we had an honest exchange of opinions. My good feelings didn't last long, though, for some weeks later, our missionary supervisor came to town to meet with my colleague and me individually. I was shown a letter my colleague had written to friends in Tennessee in which he accused me of not believing in Jesus as the Son of God or in his miracles. The letter led to my being terminated for "doctrinal ambiguity." I attempted to explain my position, which was much more nuanced than to say I did not believe in the miracles. I said that it was possible that the miracle stories were adapted or even created in the early church. The administrators said that my position was unacceptable because it violated the denomination's doctrinal statement in *The Baptist Faith and Message* that the Bible contained "truth without any mixture of error."[16] Furthermore, the administrators contended that my statement would lead to confusion on the mission field because nationals were not as sophisticated as US students. I was testifying to freedom, but the administrators were testifying to responsibility, though one could make a case that they were testifying to paternalism and oppression. Also, everything was subservient to the overarching objective to evangelize.

I wound up in a context more suitable to my theology and politics: Howard University School of Divinity (HUSD), where I taught for over a quarter of a century. HU is a historically Black university (an HBCU), and at HUSD were students (and professors) who were African Americans,

16. Hobbs, *Baptist Faith and Message*, 1.

Afro-Caribbeans, and Africans, as well as a few whites and Asian Americans. In this brilliant mosaic, I thrived. In my teaching, I made connections between individual salvation and social justice. For me, they are two wings on the same bird—the soaring dove that represents the Holy Spirit. Bringing together personal salvation and social justice is simply part of my testimony. Remember what I said earlier: I was born in Independence and raised at Liberty, so freedom is important to me!

I arrived at HUSD in 1991. Five years later, I was dealing with two important events in my life, one professional and the other personal: I was applying for tenure, and my first child was born. Amid those high-pressure activities, I "lost my faith." It seemed that my belief in God tumbled like a house of cards. My wife Joy sometimes jokes that most fathers see their newborn children and exclaim, "There is a God!" But when I saw my elder daughter born, I said, "I don't know if there is a God!" Well, it did not happen exactly like that. I think that I felt keenly the pressure of tenure application and fatherhood anticipation, and my anxiety was too much for my faith structure, so I jettisoned it. I did not consider that such questions would be welcome in a Baptist church, so my wife, our new baby, and I began to worship among Friends, that is the Religious Society of Friends—Quakers—where they had silent worship. In that context, I began to rebuild my faith structure, recovering a sense of the presence of God. I cannot pinpoint one moment in which I regained my faith—not my promotion with tenure, not the birth of our second child. It was just a growing certainty of a loving presence in the universe.

Another major turning point began with the death of my mother in 2011.[17] It really shook my foundations, sending my life in upheaval. First, I took the buy-out (called the PRP, Phased Retirement Program) at HU in 2012 and retired in 2017. I felt that God was calling me to Kenya to teach in a Quaker seminary there.[18] From 2011 to 2015, I taught short courses three times in Kenya. In the first two trips, I felt God calling, but by the third trip, I did not. I had passed my sixtieth birthday, and that sense of clearness about teaching in Africa was gone.

---

17. My parents died forty years apart, almost to the day. My father died October 13, 1971, my mother October 4, 2011.

18. That seminary is Friends Theological College, Kaimosi, Kenya. There are more Quakers in Kenya than any other country in the world, including the United States. East African Quaker worship is programmed, that is, they have sermons and music, unlike unprogrammed Quakers, who worship in silence.

The second upheaval was that in 2013 I separated from my wife of nineteen years, moving to a friend's house up for sale, then guest housing at HUSD, and finally rented space near my wife and two daughters. After counseling, my wife and I decided to reconcile, though we separated again, and reconciled again. I also became a Baptist minister again, called to serve as an interim pastor (also called "transitional minister") through Transition Ministries of American Baptist Churches of the United States of America (TM-ABCUSA). I have served churches in Wisconsin, New York, and Connecticut. I am writing this paragraph from Suffield, Connecticut, where I am serving as interim pastor of Second Baptist Church. (I will soon finish this position and begin another one in Rhode Island.)

Interpreting Scripture

My own vocation as an interim pastor describes one aspect of the personal context in which I see the Scripture. First, I am a clergyperson, ordained first among Southern Baptists and then among American Baptists (which until 1950 was known as the Northern Baptist Convention[19]). I interpret the Bible to undergird religious faith, but sometimes I interpret the Bible to under*mine* religious faith. Ideally, I undergird faith in the God of liberation; I undermine faith in the God of oppression. In other words, I testify to liberation. At least, it is my intention to do so. True liberation comes when I can become aware where I testify to oppression as well as liberation—and various admixtures of such.

As a "transitional minister," I am more sensitive to the transitions that church members are experiencing in the times between "settled pastors." But people are always in transition, and churches are always in transition. And even the Scripture itself is in transition. Certainly, it was written millennia ago, but we have no original manuscript of any writing in the Bible. All we have are copies of copies of copies of copies, and all these copies don't agree. And manuscripts continue to be uncovered, and textual critical readings continue to be discussed. Thus, for example, the most widely used critical edition of the Greek New Testament (Nestle-Aland) is in its twenty-eighth edition, and a twenty-ninth edition is in preparation. Furthermore, new Bible translations (and paraphrases), like the New NRSV Updated Edition (NRSV-ue), are available; my co-author participated in the review of Philemon and Colossians. The Bible itself testifies to transition!

19. See Sunnyside Baptist Church, "Origins and Development."

The second factor is that I am a religious scholar. Upon retirement from HUSD, I received the title of Professor Emeritus of New Testament Language and Literature. I bring knowledge of various interpretations of the biblical text. We believe that Mark was the first Gospel written and that it was used in the writing of Matthew and Luke, along with a hypothetical sayings source often referred to as "Q." I interpret the Bible using psychological theory or narrative criticism.[20] People often interpret the Bible with much feeling. They project much emotion into their interpretation. How does the Bible move them? Why does it? What are interpreters—whether scholars or lay—projecting onto the text? How is their social location affecting their interpretation?

Further questions arise: Is the reader speaking from an academic or ecclesial context? If academic, is the reader affiliated with a religiously affiliated school? If ecclesial, does the religious body self-identify as progressive or conservative? How have those in authority in that religious body interpreted Scripture? More personally, how have authority figures in the reader's life (pastor or Sunday school teacher, college or seminary teacher, or other trusted adult) interpreted Scripture? What is the reader's relationship to a religious body? Who is testifying? The body (through the individual)? The individual? The local congregation? How is the congregation affiliated?

What is the reader's politics, their racial identification? What sex or gender does the reader identify with? What class? What religion does the reader profess? In an essay, "Toward a Psycho-social Reading of the Fourth Gospel," I coined the term "psycho-social location," which refers to the emotional needs the reader has.[21] (Unfortunately, the term never caught on. Indeed, I did not use it outside of that article. I think that it has potential, and maybe I will revive it—after nearly thirty years since I used the term.)

Questions continue: How is the reader using the Bible to exercise power? What power does the reader have? What are they seeking to do with the Bible? To what do they testify? To whom? Why? We could continue the questions forever. These questions help to focus our inquiry into a reader's personal context.

What about a text's context? A text's context consists of historical and literary contexts, as stated above. Historical context refers to what was going on in the time in which the text was written. For example, Matt 28:18

---

20. See Newheart, *"My Name Is Legion."* Also, Newheart, "Hermeneutic of Human Dignity," 131–49.

21. Newheart, "Toward a Psycho-Literary Reading," 43–58.

seems to indicate that the Gospel was written for Greek-speaking Jewish Christians who were evangelizing the gentiles. I say "Greek-speaking" because the Gospel was written in the Greek that was the common language of the Mediterranean world in Jesus's day. I say "Jewish" because of the many references to the Hebrew Scripture in the Gospel. I say "Christians" because it seems that the Gospel is written not to persuade people to become Christians or Jesus Christ-followers but to those who are already Christians, who already believe that Jesus is the Messiah, the Son of God (Matt 16:16). I say, "evangelizing gentiles," that is, presenting the Gospel to non-Jews because in Matt 28:18, Jesus tells the eleven disciples (the twelve minus Judas, who has killed himself, Matt 27:5) to make disciples of "all the nations," which can also be translated as "all the Gentiles." Sometimes the ancient text itself—in this case Matthew—as a historical document is a significant witness for the history behind the text, but also the text of Matthew creates a world that may not agree with the world behind the text that we can construct using external resources like archaeological discoveries like inscriptions.

Readers investigate not only historical contexts but also literary contexts. Writers formed words into sentences into paragraphs into documents that others collected together into what is known as the New Testament, which is combined with (and makes use of) the Old Testament, or Hebrew Bible, to form the Christian Bible. How do these paragraphs and sections relate to one another to create meaning? The documents are sixty-six in all—thirty-nine in the Old Testament and twenty-seven in the New Testament. (We are not satisfied with this terminology. "Old" Testament sounds like it is outmoded. Academics speak of the Hebrew Bible or Hebrew Scriptures. Some scholars speak of First and Second Testaments.[22] If we are going to talk about Hebrew Scriptures, perhaps we should also speak of the Greek Testament. We are not keen on any of these solutions so we will stick to "Old Testament" and "New Testament.")

A particular Scripture passage testifies in the context of a document. For example, the Beatitudes—"Blessed are the poor in spirit . . . (Matt 5:3–12)"—begin the Sermon on the Mount in Matt 5–7. In many ways, one interprets the entire Sermon in the context of the Beatitudes.

---

22. Sanders, "First Testament and Second," 47–49.

The Sermon is the first of five speeches in the Gospel of Matthew.[23] Jesus appears in the Gospel primarily as a teacher.[24] Certainly, he is a miracle worker (healer, exorcist, etc.), but through both word and deed, Jesus proclaims the kingdom (or reign or dominion) of God. The five speeches include the Sermon on the Mount (chs. 5–7), the Missionary Discourse (ch. 10), Parable Discourse (ch. 13), the Discourse on the Church (ch. 18), and the Woes and the Eschatological Discourse (chs. 23–25).

So often we say, "You're taking my words out of context." Of course, words are always taken out of context. Matthew 5–7 was written in Greek in the late first century CE (common era). Simply to read the Beatitudes in English in early twenty-first century US is to take them out of context. I remember when I was talking to a school administrator about a perceived lapse in communication. He said, "Let me contextualize." After his rambling monologue, I thought, "You don't need to contextualize; you just need to apologize." Context is a good thing, but it is best used when it sharpens the meaning of the passage in question. Sometimes when context is provided, that is, when a passage is contextualized, an interpreter is accused of explaining the passage away or watering it down. Context, however, serves to sharpen and clarify meaning rather than cloud or discount.

Mitzi Smith's Testimony in Context about Context

In chapter 1, I mentioned that my co-author Newheart was my first NT seminary professor at HUSD. Newheart taught me the importance of and skill of reading texts in their literary and historical contexts; he assigned a twenty-page exegetical paper in the Gospels and the Acts of the Apostles course.[25] Newheart's colleague Cain Hope Felder required a short six-page exegesis paper in his intro course, which covered the rest of the NT. Together the two instructors challenged us to spend time with the biblical

23. Sermon on the Mount, chs. 5–7; Missionary Discourse, ch. 10; Parable Discourse, ch. 13; Community Discourse, ch. 18; End Times Discourse, ch. 24–25.

24. Contra, Smith, "'Knowing More Than Is Good.'" Smith argues that we cannot separate Jesus as a teacher from his acts of justice or miracles among the people; to do so privileges teaching above acts of justice.

25. I chose to write a second twenty-page exegetical paper for extra credit (not that I needed it); my goal was to master the process. I had left the denomination that I was a member of and served for more than fifteen years to pursue my call and that meant preparation for an uncertain future. I promised God and myself to give it my best shot. There was no turning back!

passages we had chosen, to think critically and contextually about them, and attempt to write clearly, creatively, and succinctly or extensively. Felder ignited my enthusiasm for justice as a hermeneutical goal or purpose, as the *raison d'être*, of biblical interpretation for and in the Black community. I remember being in class the evening before the Million Man March that would occur in Washington, DC the next day; Felder brimmed with excitement, pride, and expectation. He had lived through many of the racial injustices we had only read about and were yet to experience in a racialized patriarchal academy, Christian church, and world. Context matters. The reader's context matters. My communities and their contexts matter. Who am I (or how have I become who I am *now*; *now* is relative) as an interpreter of biblical texts? And how does who I am and am becoming impact how I read?

I am a native daughter born to Flora Opheila Carson Smith (1927–2009) and Fred Powell Smith Sr. in Columbus, Ohio.[26] Flora was a Black native daughter of the US South, born in Cassville, Georgia, but raised in Cleveland, Tennessee, by her grandparents, Flora Jane Carson and George Carson ("Daddy George"), who were born in the nineteenth century. My great-grandmother Flora Jane, a trained nurse, helped found the hospital in Cleveland, Tennessee, for which she received no acknowledgement; she and "Daddy George," her husband, owned and worked a farm, often holding three jobs, including cooking and ironing for "white folk," which allowed them to purchase and maintain the farm. Thus, I am a daughter of the North and the South; I lived in the North most of my life; now I live in Georgia.

Growing up in Columbus, Ohio, the percentage of African Americans in the state was less than the national percentage. Like most Black children, if I didn't know I was Black before I turned four years old, I knew it when I entered elementary school. White children who invited themselves to run their hands over my braids were surprised at the softness of my hair; they expected something different. I was a third grader at a Presbyterian summer camp the first time I distinctly remember being called a n*gger.

---

26. Some readers will correctly associate my use of the adjective "native" with Richard Wright's classic book *Native Son*. Wright, an African American author who was born in a sharecropper's cabin in Mississippi and grew up in extreme poverty, first published that *Native Son* in 1940. As a recent attendee of the 2022 Wabash workshop for African diaspora scholars, Marcia Y. Riggs and Kenneth Ngwa, our facilitators, challenged us to pen our journeys in theological education in conversation with Keri Day's recent text entitled *Notes of a Native Daughter*.

We attended the Presbyterian mission called Calvary Chapel (a couple of miles from our apartment in the projects), which was led by Jack Borowski and his wife. My mother could not take us to church, so she allowed the Borowskis to pick us up in their church bus on Sunday mornings. Once we became third-graders, the large wealthy white Broad Street Presbyterian church allowed the neighborhood children (mostly Black) who attended the mission from the projects to attend their summer camp free of charge. A white girl my age named M***y befriended me, and we became insepa-rable at camp; her family attended Broad Street and served as camp coun-selors every year. We gleefully reunited every summer for several years at the camp as best friends. We defended each other when necessary from our respective bullies. She cried and told her mother when a little white boy felt the need to call me a n*gger. My best friend at the mostly white elementary school I attended was also a little white girl; her name was Cathy. Neither friend ever visited me at my home, but I was invited to each of their homes once. I recall how excited I was when M***y's family invited me to their home for lunch. They lived up north in the suburb of Upper Arlington. To me, they were rich! I greatly anticipated feasting on steak. But to my disap-pointment we ate Campbell soup and bologna sandwiches. I thought to myself, "I could have had this at home," but I was happy to spend time with M***y outside of camp. In a world mapped by race and social economic status, such friendships tend to dissolve by junior high school; once close friends might hesitantly wave at one other from the distance, if they ever *see* each other again.

The second time a white person called me a n*gger I was a junior in high school working a part-time job in a retail credit agency where I filed papers and did a little typing. A young white woman had nothing better to do but step in front of me and call me a n*gger while I stood at the filing cabinet placing documents into the appropriate folders. My extremely shy sixteen-year-old self was momentarily stunned but said nothing. Rumor in the office was that she was having an affair with the boss, that fact and that he was a white male assured me that he would not be interested in what I might say. Most African American children experience racism as early as preschool, if not before.

Black people who migrated north carried in their bodies trauma, epis-temologies, faith, and survival skills—improvisation, "making do," hope, rituals, resilience, and care for family and community. Mommy, living in a two-bedroom apartment with three small children, returned to the South to bring "Daddy George" north after great-grandmother Flora died. Mom slept on the couch and gave him her bed until he died. Mommy was a Christian, a daughter of the Methodist Episcopal church, but more importantly, she, not Jesus or the church, was my first mentor and example of how a godly person conducted herself; she modeled an admirable work ethic, unconditional love, and justice. Mom believed in treating her patients at the St. Luke's hospital where she worked in Cleveland, Ohio, as if they were her own people.[27] She never expressed defeat, not to us or out aloud anyway, despite the many traumas or illnesses she suffered from childhood until death. When she was a toddler my mother fell headfirst into a fireplace. She and Nellie (her older sister) were struggling for the right to play with the same doll, but Nellie let go. The healing process was long and painful—physically and emotionally; teachers can be as cruel as young children. Mommy also suffered from narcolepsy in high school, and yet she was her high school's valedictorian. Just as she had learned, mommy taught her children how to keep putting one foot in front of the other when tempted to give up. She believed in prayer but not without seeking, expecting, or doing what we could do to make a way out of no way. Mommy worked hard and smartly, often in physical pain and without Obamacare. When she could no longer extend her hamstrings to walk, she said to us one day, "when I was walking, you couldn't tell which corner my dress tail went around last." Translation: ya'll movin' too slow. Friends and family know me as a fast walker. In many ways, I am my mother's daughter.

Before Mommy could no longer walk, she received a first-place beautification award for the flower garden she planted in our modest front yard in the projects. She was the youngest woman in the diverse neighborhood women's garden club, and at four years old, I accompanied her. "In search of our mother's gardens, I found my own," wrote Alice Walker.[28] When we had little to eat, Mommy sent us outside to nearby fields to pick polk salad and dandelion greens.

My mother loved her community, but she was a no-nonsense woman who didn't care for gossip and had no time for idle talk. She sometimes shared her homemade chili or peanut butter cookies—her fish and

27. St. Luke's Hospital was a historic hospital formerly located in the Woodland Hills neighborhood of Cleveland, Ohio. The building was constructed in 1927–29, with later additions between 1940 and 1970. In 1999 the hospital closed off its level 2 trauma center, and the hospital shut down the rest of its surgical and medical services later that summer.

28. Walker, *In Search of Our Mothers' Gardens*, 243.

loaves—with some of the neighborhood children, even if she wasn't sure where our next meal might come from.

My mother's grandparents read the Bible to her and her older sister Nellie e-v-e-r-y night in the King's English. As a young adult I sometimes giggled to myself when I heard my mother pray in the King's English too. My mother was a trained classical pianist, singer and orator. She shared with us that she once turned down an opportunity to travel with Louis Armstrong's band; she didn't feel comfortable traveling alone with a group of men. I cannot sing; she said I am tone deaf. But I learned that, like my mother, I could excel in foreign language studies. She studied Latin and French for two years each in her Black segregated high school in Cleveland, Tennessee. At Columbia Union College (CUC) I was the only female student in a predominantly white male (one Black male student) Greek class and earned the highest grade (me and the assistant dean of the girls' dormitory, a mature Jamaican woman who audited the course). I studied more Greek and added Hebrew in my MDiv program at HUSD. Post-graduation, I remained another year at HUSD and studied Middle Egyptian Hieroglyphs, Latin, and German and French reading simultaneously in preparation for a second round of applications to three PhD programs. Harvard accepted me; no school in the South did. It is important that we share our rejections, as we are able, because so many people who experience it think they are the only one and therefore the problem is with them. All human beings share the experience of rejection, whether it is (mis)attributed to God (e.g., Cain's offering, Gen 4:3–5) or to oppressive systems and structures, cultural biases, and unjust policies and practices.

As one trained in oratory in her segregated Black high school in the South, my mother taught us to memorize and recite, particularly poems that told a story. Her favorite was "Kentucky Bell." She coached me to learn "St. Peter at the Gate." I still recall, imperfectly, some of its lines:[29]

> St. Peter stood guard at the golden gate,
> With solemn mien and air sedate,
> When up to the top of the golden stair,
> A man and a woman ascending there,
>
> The woman was tall, and lank, and thin,
> With a scraggy beardlet upon her chin.
> The man was short, and thick, and stout,

29. Smiley, "St. Peter at the Gate."

. . .
The choirs in the distance the echoes awoke,
And the man kept still while the woman spoke.

"O thou who guards the gate," said she,
"We two came hither, beseeching thee . . .

If you guessed that St. Peter had pity on the man and let him through the pearly gate, you are correct. The wife, on the other hand, was "ushered to the regions below." Not until much later in life did I realize what a patriarchal chauvinistic mess it was!

Octavia Butler wrote in her book *Parable of the Sower*, "God is Change."[30] She further asserts that "God is Power—Infinite, Irresistible, Inexorable, Indifferent. And yet, God is Pliable—Trickster, Teacher, Chaos, Clay. God exists to be shaped. God is Change."[31] Butler has a point. All our constructions of God, all interpretations, are contextual and contingent. The idea of God as Change helps us to recognize and analyze change, to adapt to change, to resist change, to engender change, and to be the change we need and the world needs, against all odds. Perhaps, understanding God as Change reminds us we are not alone as things change; God will help us adapt to good and just Change, to resist ungodly and unjust Change, and to know the difference. We are usually miles behind God, looking at God's heels and backside, never catching up but always, if we choose, in pursuit of God and the Change required to be what God created us to be and do and to embody and practice the self-love, neighbor-love, justice, and mercy of God. Butler wrote "All that you touch, you Change. All that you Change, Changes you. The only lasting truth is Change. God is Change."[32]

While my mother was socialized and baptized, like most women and men of her generation (and of mine), to uncritically and unwittingly love patriarchy, she did not worship at its altar. Nor was she enslaved to it. She held the Bible closely but not so tightly that she feared change or refused to change and think differently than she was taught. Her religious formation did not prevent my mother from enthusiastically supporting my call to ministry and preaching when the church and the apostle Paul challenged it. The Bible was not her God, and neither was the church, although she loved both. I witnessed this firsthand in the ways she treated her children,

30. Butler, *Parable of the Sower*, 3, 17, 25, 77, 79.

31. Butler, *Parable of the Sower*, 25.

32. Butler, *Parable of the Sower*, 79.

her family, and other people. I remember calling my mother as I struggled with my call to ministry; I believed without a doubt that God called me to go and be educated to fulfill my call, but for what type of ministry I did not know. I just knew I was not supposed to limit myself.

But I did not realize the ways that I was in fact limiting myself. When I matriculated at CUC in Takoma Park, Maryland in 1981, I insisted on the same program of study that the men were taking, which included homiletics and ancient Greek. Ironically, I also argued in a paper I was writing for my first-year English class that women should not be ordained to pastoral ministry. My first "draft" of the paper earned a D. I met with the professor and told him I found myself unexpectedly struggling as I wrote the paper with what I thought I believed. He returned my paper and told me to re-write it. In the process of rewriting the paper, I telephoned my mother to ask her what she thought about women's ordination to pastoral ministry. Her opinion mattered. It's strange that I was struggling with the issue of women's ordination but had no idea what type of ministry God was calling me to. But as I typed that sentence, it occurred to me, for the first time, that perhaps God was preparing me to write about issues differently than I had been taught, and through writing, I would challenge injustice and oppression. My mother's response to the question about women's ordination shocked me. She was raised to believe that a woman should only preach in the absence of a man; she should not be ordained to pastoral ministry. Although my mother was socialized to believe women should not preach, she transcended that oppressive socialization in her absolute support of my calling—not one negative or discouraging word parted her lips. She encouraged me to preach and made sure I made it to college to study theology. God's call on my life trumped her Christian patriarchal formation.

In my revised paper on women's ordination, which earned an A minus, I argued that we must read Paul's command for women to be silent in church in the larger literary and historical context of 1 Corinthians and what was happened among the Corinthian believers. It was an *ad hoc* prohibition and not a universal one. That was in 1981. Today, I am more like my mother. I believe God has called me. Paul and I may be at odds, but God and I are not. I do not need Paul's ancient writing to the Corinthian believers to confirm my calling. I was there when God called, and I responded.

Mommy believed in formal education and in God; she nudged me to earn a law degree (I wish I had listened) and later a PhD, long before I imagined it for myself. In high school she had two years of French and two years of Latin. I took no languages in my segregated diverse high school of students from working-class and poor families. My mother earned a two-year degree in nursing in the South. I was the first in my immediate family to earn a bachelor's and a master's degree and the only one to earn a PhD to date.

As Flora's native daughter and a Black cisgender heterosexual woman biblical scholar who centers justice and Black women, our diaspora communities and beyond, I do not regard myself as "learning to pass" in the way that Keri Day testifies of her academic journey.[33] I do not masquerade as something or someone I am not. I do think—strike that, I know—that the academic guild is hostile to those who resist or refuse to pass (i.e., to privilege and fetishize whitened[34] scholars/ship, textbooks, and methodologies/approaches to reading Scripture and to marginalize or ignore those of Black and brown scholars). When I entered the doctoral program at Harvard, I had the opportunity to learn from a Black biblical scholar, Professor Allen Callahan; this was and remains relatively rare for Africana biblical scholars to be situated in institutions where they can mentor Black doctoral students. Thus, not one Black scholar sat on my dissertation committee. Our professors are predominantly white men and women who center whiteness. When we graduate, we must clear our throats and recover our voices. Not until five years after beginning my teaching career did I have the space to self-reflect and discover my voice. To find my voice is to break my silence in favor of justice and against injustice amidst the noise that would silence my

33. Day, *Notes of a Native Daughter*. She states the following: "I benefit economically from elite structures within the theological context. However, as a black woman, I also experience a kind of loss that I describe as 'learning to pass.' In theological education, learning to pass means learning how to perform intellectual mastery within white institutions. It means mastering and teaching the white 'normative' discourses and figures as well as those treated in more peripheral ways, without much choice in the matter" (37).

34. I use the term *whitened* as opposed to *white* because white culture is treated as nonexistent, rendered invisible and normalized as such. Thus, dominant white scholars/hip pretends, implicitly or explicitly, to be objective, nonideological, non-contextual, and superior to overtly contextual epistemologies, scholarship and approaches to biblical interpretation. So that doing legitimate biblical scholarship is the performance of whiteness. Some dominant scholars are so bold as to say that the use of overtly cultural, contextual and/or ideological approaches to interpretation do not constitute biblical studies. When we were seeking a publisher for *Toward Decentering the New Testament*, an editor at a conservative press told me that the book was not an introductory text. Obviously, we disagreed and rejected her claim. Often both white and nonwhite readers and interpreters acquiesce or submit to the performance of whiteness.

dissent against centering whiteness. Patricia Hill Collins writes this about Black women breaking silence:

> Silencing occurs when Black women are restrained from confronting racism, sexism, and elitism in public transcripts because doing so remains dangerous. When Black women do break silence in situations of profoundly unequal power—from that of the secretary who finally tells off her boss, to that of Anita Hill's public accusations of sexual harassment against Clarence Thomas—breaking silence represents less a *discovery* of these unequal power relations than *a breaking through* into the public arena of what oppressed groups have long expressed in private. Publicly articulating rage typically constitutes less a revelation about oppression than a discovery of voice. For African-American women as individuals, breaking silence thus represents a moment of insubordination in relations of power, of saying *in public* what had been said many times before to each other around the kitchen table, in church, at the hairdresser, or at those all-Black women's tables in student dining halls. Breaking silence in hierarchical power relations also generates retaliation from elite groups . . . Such voice challenges the legitimacy of public transcripts claiming Black female inferiority . . . [and reclaims] Black women's humanity.[35]

The position or context from which we conscientiously and strategically read sacred texts matters. It drives the interpretative agenda (everybody has one whether they admit it or not), the questions we ask in the process of interpretation, how we see what we read and how we read what we see in the biblical text and behind the biblical text (historical context). Is the darkness that the Gospel of John (and interpreters of John) characterizes as oppositional or hostile to the light coming into the world consistent with the depiction of darkness in Gen 1:1–31 (cf. John 1:5; 8:12; 12:35–36), where God's creative word is conceived in the maternal womb that is the darkness and the waters that covered the earth at creation? Is darkness always evil and oppositional to light? If God is pre-existent, did God create darkness? Who made darkness something to be feared? At creation the darkness welcomed the light, made space for light, took turns covering the atmosphere by showing up as night. Darkness cradles us to sleep. But darkness and blackness have been constructed as the enemy of light and as evil by those who control the narratives. In the ancient Greek, the word translated darkness (ἡ σκοτία) in Gen 1:5 is grammatically feminine. Darkness, if created

---

35. Collins, *On Fighting Words*, 50–51.

by God, was with God when God created day and night, sun, moon and stars, and all living things. The darkness allows many far away stars to shine brightly and to be seen without the aid of a telescope.

My mother raised us to pay attention to details.[36] My training as a legal secretary and certified legal assistant required that I notice the details. We can all develop the skill of seeing and analyzing the details. Attention to detail—to what is and is not present, to where things are located and how they are connected, to patterns, to the significant and the seemingly insignificant, to what is noticeable with each re-reading—is a learned skill for most of us. It requires initiative, a belief in one's ability to see and read differently and contextually, because we are different as readers and one human being can never see it all.[37] It requires that we trust in the payoff from the time we spend reading, re-reading, re-reading, re-reading in context, re-reading with new and different questions, and re-reading through new experiences, with diverse conversation partners (other humans or diverse voices in different resources).

Theological education is still overwhelmingly white and male. If we think of the typical biblical studies classroom as an ecosystem—a space where diverse and interdependent life forms or living organisms dynamically co-exist in an environment, most lack the biodiversity necessary for a healthy ecosystem. The syllabi, the required and recommended textbooks, the students, the instructor, the assignments, and so forth all can contribute to creating a biodiverse ecosystem where life can thrive. What must die for all to flourish?

It is still rare for a seminary or divinity school student to enter a biblical studies classroom where the professor is a Black woman. I was the first full-time tenure-track Black woman NT scholar at Ashland Theological Seminary. I was also the first full-time tenure-track biblical scholar with primary residence in the Detroit Center/Campus where I taught both testaments, including ancient Hebrew and Greek languages and Black church studies courses. I was told that taking that job would be career suicide. I am my mother's child; I survived. I taught numerous courses and published four books and many essays while at Ashland. We all must start somewhere, and opportunities are few. At Ashland-Detroit, 95 to 100 percent of

36. The devil and the divine are in the details! says Newheart.

37. This point has to do with community, Paul's point about the body of Christ (1 Cor 12:12–26; see also Rom 12:3–8).

my students were Black women. When I taught a course in Ashland, Ohio, in the early years, 99 to 100 percent of students were white.

As a Black woman, how could I not privilege the voices, experiences, traditions, and the artifacts of the Black community to which I belong, as well as the injustices we face daily? When we start teaching, we teach the way we were taught. No matter how well-meaning or accomplished our teachers, we must often teach better and/or differently than we were taught. My biblical studies teachers were excellent, and they were predominantly men (Black and white men) and some were white women teaching in a different context from those where I taught and teach and with other foci and expertise.

At Ashland, I remembered how much I resonated with womanism and how it challenged me. I took my first womanist course from Dr. Kelly Brown Douglas at HUSD. We read Douglas's book manuscript *Sexuality and the Black Church* and Emilie Towne's *Breaking the Fine Rain of Death*, among other womanist texts. Those two texts impacted me most; Douglas's book challenged the way I had been theologically shaped by conservative Black Christianity to demonize LGBTQI+ persons and to view silence and shame as the most sacred approach to sexuality. Towne's text read the book of Joel in conversation with health care disparities in the United States. Our family watched as my mother suffered under that oppressive reality. Also, in the mid-1980s at The Ohio State University I wrote my master's thesis on the dismal statistics of cancer incidence and mortalities rates among Black peoples in Ohio counties with the largest Black populations. I discovered correlations between Black lower cancer incidence rates (than whites) but Black higher mortality rates (than white people) and access to state-of-the-art health care facilities, racism, sexism, and poverty. Womanist and linguist Geneva Smitherman argues that a womanist is an "African American woman who is rooted in the Black community and committed to the development of herself and the entire community."[38] Rootedness in the Black community demands opposition to the injustices the most vulnerable in the community face. Collins argues that we must remain oppositional [to oppressive dominant discourses and structures, to injustice], which "involves challenging the constructs, paradigms, and epistemologies or bodies of knowledge that have more power, authority, and/or legitimacy

---

38. Smitherman, "Womanist Looks at the Million Man March," 104.

than Black feminist [or womanist] thought."[39] This oppositionality is not an achieved static existence but a "state of becoming."[40]

Like Katie Cannon and Keri Day, an HBCU and my Black family and community formed me. This is not to say Harvard had no significant impact; it did. The first paper I wrote as a doctoral student that centered the Black people, our traditions, artifacts, and Christology, was written in Allen Callahan's African American Biblical Interpretation course at Harvard. Callahan arranged for some students in the course to present their papers at a Popular Culture conference. I unapologetically explored how Black enslaved people understood Jesus and *salvation history* in the Spirituals differently from *heilsgeschicte* theorized by the German scholar Hans Conzelmann. I published that essay ten years later, in a volumed Thomas Slater edited, *Afrocentric Interpretations of the New Testament Epistles Hebrew, James, Jude, Peter, John, and Revelation: Things That Black Scholars See That White Scholars Do Not*. But I published an essay on "'Slavery and the Early Church" before entering Harvard, as a master's student, in the *African American Jubilee Bible* (ed. Dr. Cain Hope Felder).

Our work must remain oppositional to oppressive whiteness and injustice. I am "involved in the work [my] soul must have"[41] and that my community needs; if others find it useful, I am grateful. As previously mentioned, some publishers told us that our book *Toward Decentering the New Testament: A Reintroduction* (Cascade 2018) is not an introductory text. I disagreed. Dissent (even of oppressive, violent and annihilating biblical texts, including characterizations of God) can disrupt the status quo, or put a dent in its tenacious shell, and perhaps eventually transform it. There are subtle and not so subtle forces at work to silence dissent against oppression, domination, marginalization, monopolization and other forms of injustice. Such powers, Renita Weems asserts, attempt to silence

> one's commitments as a professor [and student], [and encourage us] to read the Bible through the eyes of the powerful, the winners, the white gaze. But . . . there is no going back. We cannot unknow what we now know [and will learn] about police killings of Black women and men, the rise of white supremacy [and so on]. There is no return to a precritical period of reflecting on the discipline, the Bible, and its use in the hands of extremists. We have the

---

39. Collins, *On Fighting Words*, 88.
40. Collins, *On Fighting Words*, 89.
41. Walker, *In Search of Our Mothers' Gardens*, 241.

responsibility to think and teach better than we have been trained
. . . we cannot avoid the need to be self-reflexive about our location
and our training, because . . . readers and the act of reading itself
are not so innocent.[42]

I am a survivor of childhood sexual abuse. My essay, "'He Never Said a
Mumbalin' Word': A Womanist Perspective of Crucifixion, Sexual Violence
and Sacralized Silence" begins with the story of my abuse when I was eight
years older or younger; it is that part of my story, my context that compelled
me to say 'yes' to the invitation to write the essay.[43]

I am an ordained minister and have worked in the church since I was
a teenager. I was ordained as a local elder in three SDA congregations (Columbus, Ohio; Washington, DC; and Bladensburg, Maryland), served as
a youth pastor for a DC Presbyterian Church, and as executive minister
at Oak Grove AME Church (Detroit). I began the ordination process as
an itinerant elder in the AME church while at Oak Grove and completed
it at St. Matthews AME in Detroit. Thus, I have served in three different
denominations with diverse theological commitments and rituals. When I
was invited to serve at Faith Presbyterian Church in southeast Washington,
DC, the pastor Rev. Dr. Bernice Parker Jones asked me if I would be okay
with participating in baptisms by sprinkling. I believed all my baptized life
that baptism by immersion was the only way to perform the ritual, but as
I reflected I changed my mind. They are both human-constructed rituals
and one is as efficacious as the other in their different contexts. I must say,
however, that a naïve sixteen-year-old emerging from the frigid waters of
a SDA baptismal pool shivering can be convinced that the Spirit filled her!
That was my testimony for years.

Dr. Gene Rice solicited testimonies of the students in his introduction
to the Old Testament/Hebrew Bible course. At the beginning of the course,
Rice asked students to share a favorite Scripture. At the end of the course
on the final exam, he asked students to write about how the meaning of
the Scripture had change after knowing more about its context. The text I
shared was Jer 32:17: "Ah Lord God! It is you who made the heavens and
the earth by your great power and by your outstretched arm! Nothing is
too hard for you" (NRSV). Many days that verse encouraged my soul when
I faced what seemed like impossible odds. But reading it in the context of
the Babylonian siege of Jerusalem and the promise of God to the prophet

42. Weems, "'To Think Better,'" 276.
43. Smith, "'He Never Said a Mumbalin' Word.'"

Jeremiah that the Chaldeans/Babylon would conquer Jerusalem was like polishing a diamond in the rough. In almost the same Divine breath, YHWH told Jeremiah to buy the property in the land of Benjamin that his cousin would offer to sell him, knowing that Jerusalem would fall to the Babylonians and he would be taken captive (Jer 32:6–8). Just as YHWH instructed him, Jeremiah legally purchased the land, executing and sealing the proper deeds of purchase, and storing them in vessels that would preserve their integrity for a long time; God promised the land would be restored in a distant future (32:9–15). It is in this context, that Jeremiah declared in prayer that nothing is too difficult for the God who made the heavens and the earth and whose love is unwavering (32:16–18). In the face of sure destruction of the land, Jeremiah performs an act of faith and hope in YHWH to do what is unimaginable; there are no sticks to make a fire, no straw to make bricks, no coins to increase, and no meal in the jar. I once told some of my students in Detroit that we could compare Jerusalem at that time to the city of Highland Park, Michigan (a suburb of Detroit). God told Jeremiah to go purchase property in Highland Park. The city that once boasted of the best jobs, schools, hospitals, and municipal services of any in the United States, but today it is the site of the worst poverty and suffering in the United States. The disinvestment of Ford Motor and other companies led to the slow decline of Highland Park (and Flint and Pontiac, Michigan); the poverty rate is about 52 percent and the mostly Black population is under 15,000. The highway system also plowed through Black neighborhoods like Highland Park, Detroit, and Hamtramck. The few residents that remain in Highland Park cannot afford to move, to buy property elsewhere; their closest neighbors are abandoned rundown homes; they have no fire department, no police presence, no protection. Is any anything too hard for God? Some days, it is no longer a rhetorical question but an indictment, and that's alright! God can handle it.

Learning the skill of biblical interpretation is a journey. After a student complaint early in my career that I expect students to write like me, like a biblical scholar, I started using at least one student paper (with the student's permission and anonymously) as a model for writing a biblical interpretation paper. I tell students that I am not looking for perfection, but I am expecting them to put forth an effort, to be open to seeing and reading differently, and that they bring their unique contexts to the process. We are all witnesses!

Newheart appends this digital painting here entitled "Context Is Everything." He used the Paint 3D program on his HP laptop to create the image.

Context Is Everything

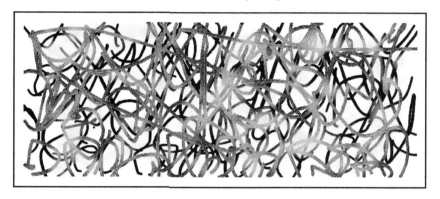

3

(New) Testament Texts as Testimony

Is it possible to write religion-inflected prose narrative that does not rest its case entirely or mainly on biblical language? Is it possible to make the experience and journey of faith fresh, as new and as linguistically unencumbered as it was to early believers, who themselves had no collection of books to rely on?

—TONI MORRISON, *THE SOURCE OF SELF-REGARD*

Testing the Texts as Testimony

THE BIBLE IS TESTIMONY. In the biblical witness all of creation—human, Divine, and inanimate testify! The Bible is a witness that contains diverse testimonies across time, space and cultures. And it compels readers across time, space and cultures to testify. From its G/genesis to or through R/revelation, it has created and continually births a multiplicity of witnesses and unique testimonies that range from faithful, to wonder-struck, to submissive, to ambivalent, to suspicious, to horror-struck, to traumatizing, to dissenting.

The assertion that the Bible testifies is complex. The Bible in translation/interpretation—primarily whitened translations/interpretations and by white cisgender male scholars—testifies about the translator (and vice versa), perhaps as much as it does, or more so, about the text. Or can the two be separated and to what degree? The Bible is simultaneously the testimony of various dominant white (or diverse within a homogeneity) cisgender male biblical scholars. Although, the translators-interpreters invited to participate in the review of the NRSV were more diverse than ever before in terms of race, ethnicity, gender, and sexuality, in most respects, if not all, the language, the testimony, of the updated edition, the *NRSVue*, remains unchanged. The required template, the proto-text, or *uber*-language on which it relies is a whitened text and language. Other colorful guests were seated at the proverbial table, but the white table cloth, the menu and the utensils remained the same. Power determines whose testimonies are shared and heard, how or if they are constructed, shared, and heard, when and where, and who hears and shares them. What communities and who within the community has power over testimonies?

Texts as testimonies arise out of (are written, produced and shaped within and by) particular and diverse communities. They reflect the cultures, concerns, and experiences of those communities, which may or may not coincide with the culture, interests and challenges of other ancient and contemporary communities. Texts are used in community, and in reading them and interpreting them, they become a part of that larger community not bound by space and time. To texts are attributed authority within communities, by communities, and transcending communities through a F/force larger than human communities. Many of the New Testament documents are epistles, and many of them refer to "we" and "you [all]," indicating a consciousness of community and the testimonies that arise or are shared within them that form a basis of knowing and unknowing. Sybille Krämer argues the following:

> epistemic dependence is a constituent element of the human epistemological situation. We rely on being informed through others in order to be able to know anything at all; and this is true not only in the early years of our childhood, but even in the elaborated forms of scholarly work. Thinking and knowing are terms of fundamentally *cooperative actions*. The contemporary epistemological debate over testimony thus radically calls into question the ideas of epistemic individualism and epistemic autonomy.[1] [author's emphasis]

Texts as testimony constitute a form of knowledge and power. By *texts* we mean primarily, but not exclusively biblical texts—those sixty-six books in collections commonly called *The Bible*: thirty-nine in the Old Testament (OT) and twenty-seven in the NT. The OT contains the Law, the Prophets,

---

1. Krämer, "Epistemic Dependence and Trust," 248–49.

and the Writings. The NT consists of the Gospels and Acts of the Apostles, epistles or letters, and the Apocalypse or book of Revelation. The divisions of the NT are based on those of the OT. We, however, also encourage students to expand the canon to include the apocryphal texts and other sacred texts. Newheart has stated that the sacred canon should be expanded to include Martin Luther King Jr.'s *Letter from Birmingham Jail,* and Smith, to her surprise, agrees.

The process of canonization was a process of testifying. Segments of the church were testifying that the canonical texts were inspired and/or authoritative. They stimulated collective religious experience, beyond individual piety. They grounded people in community, and not necessarily an inclusive community.

These documents communicate and facilitate religious experience, or the experience of the religious, so that the recipients may experience much the same type of religious experience and use the same language. The apostle Paul often admonishes the Corinthian believers to imitate him as he imitates Christ (1 Cor 11:1). Sometimes divisions are reported or occur within the community, and the author is writing to heal those divisions *and* to establish and/or solidify this authority. The writing of the document rhetorically and performatively extends the community and sets or constructs boundaries, often between insiders and outsiders whom Paul, for example, considers either spiritually enslaved and free (Gal 4–5). Nevertheless, for whatever reason, the writer attempts to empower the recipients. The author is writing both to gain and maintain power within the community and for the community in (or against) the world. Communication is always an act of power, power over and power with. We are writing this book to extend power or influence in terms of embracing disruptive and creative interpretation and the power and agency of others. Power over? We want to impact people. I (Newheart) want them to think that I'm a knowledgeable person, a powerful person even. However, I am not writing to make disciples for myself. I am not constructing a school of interpretation. We want people to feel empowered, that when they pick up a Bible, they can interpret it in a responsible, relevant, and contextually satisfactory way. We also want to equip readers with the skills (and perhaps confidence) to lead their religious communities (and other interested persons) in performing biblical interpretation. We want to build up the common good.

Testifying is an act of re-membering, of giving voice and power to collective or shared experiences, traditions, and concerns of the past and the present. François Hartog states, "The witness is a central figure of human communities. Through his [her or their] intercession, one may connect the past and the present: the past of what took place and the present of its attestation."[2] The witness through her testimony asserts that she was present, she saw *and* heard, and she says what she saw *and* heard. Hartog further asserts that the conjunction *and* "is fundamental. Indeed, what is it that conducts or compels this passage from seeing to saying [or experiencing and saying], what is the constitutive act of the [witness's very being? To speak—and to be ready to speak again to someone as there is no testimony without one to whom it is told?]"[3] What are the practices or reasons and impact of testimonies? Some of the practices and reasons for testimonies are exclusively religious; the religious shapes the witness. Hartog argues that "[T]he revealed religions have needed [the witness] and have reserved him an important place. This is true of Judaism, of Islam and even more so of Christianity since the witness is the very foundation of the Christian faith, and the history of Salvation is that of the propagation of a testimony."[4] However, the religious witnesses, particularly in the biblical text, have been limited to men or the male perspective, even when the religious and the juridical interconnect. The Torah required two or three male witnesses to convict a woman or man of adultery (Deut 19:15). Testimony in the biblical text is patriarchal and often elitist. The elite, but not only the elite, owned enslaved persons. Enslaved persons could only testify or be witnesses when subjected to torture; from the enslaver's perspective, the truth could not otherwise be extracted from the enslaved. The truth lay dormant in the body of the enslaved until it became necessary for the enslaver or masters to awaken it through violence for the benefit of enslavers or masters.

Testimonies reflect the social concerns (or lack thereof) of the communities or persons who testify. The Old Testament witness normalizes or takes for granted the ownership of slaves. When God calls Abram, God does not demand that he liberate his enslaved property, but they are counted among all his possessions and are forced to accompany him as he responds to God's call (Gen 12:1–9). Enslavement is also taken for granted and the violence of it normalized in the decalogue where God charges God's people to remember how God rescued them from enslavement in the land of Egypt. In remembering, the people are commanded to rest on

2. Hartog, "Presence of the Witness," 3.
3. Hartog, "Presence of the Witness," 3.
4. Hartog, "Presence of the Witness," 3.

the seventh day of week, the Sabbath. This Sabbath rest is extended to all of their property, including their male and female slaves (Exod 10:9; Deut 5:14–15). Further they are commanded not to covet their neighbor's property, including their male and female slaves (Exod 20:17; Deut 5:21b). The decalogue also commands that the people of God refrain from giving false testimony (Deut 5:20).

One of the ordinances that God gave to Moses focuses on the connection between testimonies and justice (Exod 23:1–3). God's people are not to be the bearers of false testimonies; they shall not collude or collaborate with the majority and/or "the wicked to act as a malicious witness" (Exod 23:1–2a). When anyone is called as a witness to give formal testimony in a court proceeding, they are not to "side with the majority so as to pervert justice; nor shall you be partial to the poor in a lawsuit" (Exod 23:2b–3). The prophets in Israel can be both false and true witnesses (1 Kgs 13:1–34; 22:13–18).

The prophets are YHWH's witnesses. Through the prophets, YHWH testifies against the transgressions of God's people and the nations (Mic 1:2). The prophets are witnesses who often expose and lament the creation of poverty and injustice inflicted upon the poor and the vulnerable by the powerful and wealthy (Mic 3:1–12). Although the biblical text depicts YHWH as the God who testifies, sometimes it is the biblical text (the writers) that testifies, that makes the claim "thus says YHWH" (see Isa 41:22; 43:10; 44:8). Three times in Isa 43–44 YHWH says, "You are my witnesses" (43:10, 12; 44:8). YHWH has redeemed Jacob/Israel and called them by name (43:1). In language reminiscent of the Exodus, YHWH says, "When you pass through the waters, I will be with you; and through the rivers, they shall not overwhelm you" (43:2a). YHWH also describes himself as the one who "makes a way in the sea" (43:16) and "a way in the wilderness" (43:9). Three times Israel is told not to fear (43:1, 5; 44:8), and three times YHWH says, "I am the Lord" (43:3, 11, 15).

Witnesses, Texts, and Testimonies in the NT

In the NT, Jesus as God's Messiah is established as "the witness par excellence to the point of becoming the ultimate sacrifice."[5] From Matthew to Revelation, the NT is full of testimonies about the man Jesus, the resurrected Jesus, the Jesus Christ group or movement, and Jesus the Christ

---

5. Hartog, "Presence of the Witness," 5–6.

and/or Christ Jesus. Those testimonies claim to recall the words, deeds, miracles, and/or signs that Jesus spoke or performed when he walked the earth, as well as his shameful death by crucifixion and the empty tomb. The so-called Synoptic Gospels (Mark, Matthew and Luke) and the Gospel of John consist primarily of testimonies about the miracles or signs Jesus performed, the things he said, and his death. The writings of the apostle Paul are not concerned about the life of Jesus; they testify to the gospel of the resurrected and exalted Jesus. Hartog asserts the following:

> the entire edifice of Christianity is a matter of witnesses because it rests upon a chain of witnesses: from the first among them, John the Baptist, until the final proclamation of Jesus at the moment of the Ascension—reprise and direct echo of that which we found in the book of Isaiah. "You will be my witnesses," Jesus announces, "until the end of the earth" (Acts 1:8) . . . The church is made of a long procession of witnesses, and of witnesses of witnesses, which are at the very basis of its authority.[6]

Testimony is performance and performative, that is, there is an expectation in that consecrated space and time that people will stand and share a testimony and the testimony accomplishes or engenders something. To say that testimony is performance does not mean that it is fake, that witnesses are being deceitful or that it is not rational. No, the sermon is performance, the prayers are performance, even the announcements and collection of the offering are performance. They are public activities, often done in a ritualized fashion. But even so, such performance is performative in that it becomes a means of self-encouragement and strength and encourages others to share their testimonies or to face difficulties, to be resilient, or to behave courageously (not necessarily fearlessly). J. Stephen Kroll-Smith discusses this perspective in his article, "The Testimony as Performance: The Relationship of an Expressive Event to the Belief System of a Holiness Sect." He writes, "From the point of view of performance, testimony is a socially situated use of speech that involves rules or norms for its appropriate expression."[7]

In the Gospel of Mark, which is the only canonical Gospel identified as good news (εὐαγγέλιον) (1:1), to proclaim good news is to testify. Linked to good news in Mark's Gospel is the [human] voice crying in the wilderness, paving the way for the one who is to come (1:1–3). Similarly in Matthew's

---

6. Hartog, "Presence of the Witness," 6.

7. Kroll-Smith, "Testimony as Performance," 18.

Gospel, after the story of the survival and relocation of Joseph, Mary, and Jesus in Nazareth, John the Baptist appears as the testifying voice in the wilderness to Jesus's existence, power, and coming (Matt 3:1–11). Who is listening to John's testimony? All the Judean people went to John in the wilderness to hear John's testimony. In both Matthew and Mark, the crying voice is the witness, the one whose testimony prepares the way for another and greater Spirit anointed and Spirit-baptizing witness named Jesus. The witness of the greater witness relies on a testimony from the distant past, the prophetic witnesses (Isa 40:3; Exod 23:20; Mal 3:1). John the Baptist's testimony creates a bridge between the past and the present. When Jesus arrives, his proclamation or testimony is the "good news of God, [which is,] "The time is fulfilled, and the kingdom of God has come near; repent and believe in the good news" (1:14–15, NRSV). Jesus's testimony is oppositional or subversive to the violence and injustices of human-constructed kingdoms and empires.

The Gospel of Matthew also bears witness to fugitivity, infanticide, murder, lament, chronic generational trauma, and unresolved grief: When Herod the Great attempts to kill the baby Jesus, born king of the Jews, his parents flee after being warned by an angel (Matt 2:13–15). Mary, Joseph and their child become fugitives from violence and find refuge in Egypt. But other infants and children under the age of two and their parents cannot flee; there is no salvation for them in fugitivity. They are murdered and their families never receive justice: Rachel cannot be consoled; justice is a fugitive (Matt 2:16–18).

Jarvis Givens argues that all textbooks that Black schoolteachers wrote from the late nineteenth century to the publication of Carter G. Woodson's first textbook in 1922 included "expansive coverage of maroons, fugitive slaves, and slave insurrections . . . The objective of black education was freedom and transforming the lives of black people."[8] Givens writes the following:

> oppositional gaze of black students was made and remade through shared testimonies and personal experiences, and these memories were called on in black students' educational journeys. Writing about black witnessing, Elizabeth Alexander has argued that black people have been looking and "forging a traumatized collective historical memory" . . . In addition to forging a traumatized collective memory, black people also forged a memory of black

---

8. Givens, *Fugitive Pedagogy*, 130, 204.

fugitive life—moments where black people subverted structures of antiblack control and social technologies of terror. They witnessed black precarity as well as black people straining against their confined realities. Both sides of this phenomenon were critical for black students' interpretations of their educational encounters.[9]

As teachers of freed Black children testified about Black fugitivity, the children participated in those testimonies: they listened and watched as witnesses and *became* true witnesses to lessons and power of Black fugitivity.

In the biblical texts, we find true and false witnesses. Toward the end of Jesus's life, some chief priests and the council unsuccessfully search for false testimony (ψευδομαρτυρίαν) against Jesus, despite the many false witnesses (ψευδομαρτύρων) that volunteer their services (Matt 26:57–60). Eventually, two false witnesses with sufficiently damning testimony emerge; they testify that Jesus claimed that he would destroy God's temple (Matt 26:61). Jesus himself refuses to offer counter-testimony (καταμαρτυροῦσιν); he is silent (Matt 26:62–63). But when Jesus does speak, his words are called blasphemous and self-incriminating, so that witnesses (μαρτύρων) are no longer needed (26:65–68). Jesus began his ministry on the testimony of two voices—one in the wilderness and the other from heaven (3:3, 17), and his ministry culminates on the testimony of two false witnesses.

In the Gospels, Jesus proclaims and performs good news. Good news is contextual; what is good for one person or group (e.g., enslaved women or persons living in poverty) may not be good for others (e.g., the wealthy). In Mark, the presence of Jesus, the Holy One of God, is not good news to unclean spirits (1:21–28; cf. 5:1–20), but Jesus sometimes shows compassion on unclean spirits that he expels from the humans they inhabit and traumatize (5:12–13). When Jesus informs the Twelve that those who desire to be first must come last and serve all, I don't imagine all Twelve considered his words good news (9:33–35). Later the two brothers James and John request to sit on Jesus's right and left in glory. The request angered the other ten and prompt Jesus to basically repeat his words of reversal: whoever desires to be the greatest will serve all the others (10:35–45).

How shall we testify so that oppression in sacred testimonies is not normalized, legitimized, and replicated in our testimonies? Critical testimony that exposes, names, and deconstructs oppressive words, laws, policies, practices, and narratives *is good news* to those who are or have been oppressed and violated by harmful theologies, hermeneutics, language,

9. Givens, *Fugitive Pedagogy*, 202.

legislation, rules, practices, and histories. Jesus's teaching on divorce at Mark 10:1–13 would not be received as good news by the woman, man, or child forced to marry her rapist or who is physically, legally, or theologically forced or coerced to remain in a violent and abusive marriage or relationship. We must read against the grain, employing a deconstructive and/or oppositional justice-focused hermeneutical perspective that supports a woman, man, or child's decision to leave or to divorce an abusive partner. Abuse and violence inscribed and normalized in the Gospels or any biblical text should be met with counter-testimony that promotes intersectional love, mercy, and well-being.

In the prologue of the Gospel of Luke, the author (whom we call Luke) claims to have examined existing narratives or testimonies written by persons who had seen (and heard) for themselves what Jesus said and did (Luke 1–4; cf. Acts 1:1–8). That Luke and the other Gospels are testimonies does not make them inherently irrational or unreliable as a source of knowledge and knowledge production.

In the early second-century CE sequel to Luke's Gospel, the Acts of the Apostles, the narrative recounts twelve plus people who become witnesses, beginning in Jerusalem to the end of the earth (1:8; cf. 1:12–26); they all testify about the wonderful acts of God (2:1–11). Central to Acts and what compels the narrative is the resilient God-empowered testimony of the apostles and evangelists, particularly Peter, Saul/Paul, Stephen, Philip, and other named and unnamed apostles, prophets and teachers (see 5:33–39; 13:1–3; 18:24—19:1). Luke, as we shall call the author, assembled the existing testimonies to construct his own testimony about those who testified after Jesus's death, empty tomb, exaltation. The reconstituted Twelve and many other apostles and disciples testified about the miraculous acts of God, and particularly that God raised Jesus (Acts 1:1—2:13; 2:22–24). In Peter's speech at Pentecost, which builds upon the testimony of the prophets (e.g., Moses and David, cf. 3:20–22), he declares that "This Jesus God raised up, and of that all of us are witnesses (μάρτυρες)," (2:32, NRSV; cf. 3:13–16; 5:29–32; 8:35; 13:28–30, 37; 17:30–31). Knowledge and testimony are connected; knowledge is departed and/or received from Peter's testimony within the community (2:36). Addressing the connection between knowledge, testimony, and rationality, Krämer states the following:

> Testimony relinquishes the need for evidence [what is the evidence that God raised Jesus and exalted him?] without thereby losing its episteme distinction as a form of knowledge that is justified

with good reasons. Testimonial knowledge is not "beyond rationality", but rather it is considered a specific yet fundamental and
widely used form of rationality. But what does "rationality" mean
within a non-evidential context? At its most basic level testimonial
knowledge is an operation that connects—at the minimum—two
people with one another. Bearing witness is a cooperation between the testifer and the addressee or auditorium, who both
assume different yet complementary roles. "Testifying emerges
from the interplay of "telling" and "believing," which is allocated
to different people at different moments: the auditorium acquires
new knowledge, but is unable to verify this knowledge "first-hand,
because it is the testifer who assumes the epistemic guarantee and
responsibility for what is said through his or her [or their] speech
act of testimony. Testimonial knowledge is only possible through
the interplay of both of these roles, which includes the authority of
the testifier as well as the addressee's trust in this authority.[10]

As in the Gospel, we find in Acts testimonies considered true and authoritative, as well as false witnesses and counter-testimonies received or
treated as trustworthy. Similar to the testimony about Jesus in the Gospels,
in the Acts of the Apostles false witnesses are conjured to give false testimony against Stephen. The testimony of the false witnesses is like that presented against Jesus: "They set up false witnesses (μάρτθρας ψευδεῖς) who
said, 'This man never stops saying things against this holy place and the
law; for we have heard him say that this Jesus of Nazareth will destroy this
place and will change the customs that Moses handed on to us'" (6:13–14,
NRSV). Do you see other instances of false testimony or witnesses in the
Gospels or in Acts? What counter-testimony would you offer in your re-
reading of these biblical texts?

The idea of what constitutes a miracle as opposed to magic is contested
and depicted or treated as false testimony in the Acts narrative and by modern interpreters-translators (and in the Gospels). In Acts, the risen Jesus's
apostles perform miracles but others practice magic (see 19:11–20).[11] For
example, in the story of Paul's encounter with the enslaved Pythian proph-
etess, translators and readers refer to her as a fortune teller or diviner, both
of which are negatively construed by contemporary interpreters (16:16–
18). However, the word "diviner" is also used to describe prophets in the

---

10. Krämer, "Epistemic Dependence and Trust," 248.

11. See Knapp, "How Magic and Miracles Spread," 50–53.

OT.[12] The enslaved Pythian girl is said to possess "a spirit of divination" or it possesses her.[13] The biblical text (or the writers and/or interpreters) testifies that her powers are no match for Paul's authority or powers and that he performs an exorcism on her resulting in the spirit leaving her body. In my (Smith's) view, Paul abuses his powers when he acts to destroy her spirit simply because she *annoys* him (Acts 16:16–18; cf 1 Cor 13:1–2). Her oracle is true; her gift is effective and miraculous, otherwise her enslavers could not have made significant revenues from her powers (Acts 16:16).[14] Her gift and Paul's could have co-existed. Because Acts *testifies* or *textifies* that Paul performs a successful exorcism on the enslaved Pythian girl together with the negative and culturally-charged language used to identify her gift, readers conclude that Paul liberated her from evil and that she will subsequently live a life free of her enslavers. Her enslavers still own her, but she may be worth less to them without her valuable gift. The alternative will likely be forced prostitution, all because she dared prophesy a true Word when Paul was having a bad day!

Returning to the Gospels, the Gospel of John states that the word was with God and dwelled with or among humankind. Yung Suk Kim argues that Jesus embodied the Word, but was not equal to the Word.[15] The incarnate word is a witness. John the Baptist came as God's witness to testify about the light (John 1:6–7, 34). In John, Jesus embodies the word and is the lamb of God who testifies, but also the Hebrew Scriptures testify about Jesus as the channel of God's eternal life and salvation to the world (5:39; cf. 3:16). Can you identify other witnesses and testimonies, as well as counter-testimony in the Gospel of John?

The Epistles and Apocalypse as Testimony

Paul the apostle testifies to a direct encounter with the Risen Christ. After listing several people who are witnesses to a resurrection appearance (1 Cor 15:5–7), Paul includes himself: "Last of all, as to one untimely born, he

12. See Gafney, *Daughters of Miriam*.

13. See Bazzana, *Having the Spirit of Christ*. Bazzana argues that the language of demon possession is problematic, but he takes seriously "spirit possession" as a material reality recognizable among ancient people and modern readers. Spirits can be good, evil or morally ambiguous as neither good or evil.

14. See Smith, *Literary Construction*.

15. Kim, *Truth, Testimony and Transformation*.

appeared also to me" (15:8). Paul, however, does not describe that experience. Indeed, he changes his language from resurrection to grace. It is the grace of God toward him and with him (15:10).

Paul also talks about grace in another one of his few references to his encounter with the Risen Christ. "God, who had set me apart before I was born and called me through his grace, was pleased to reveal his Son to me, so that I might proclaim him among the Gentiles" (Gal 1:16). Paul's apostolic authority is grounded in his having seen the Risen One. He writes, "Am I not free? Am I not an apostle? Have I not seen Jesus our Lord?" (1 Cor 9:1). Paul's testimony is authoritative because it grounds his authority in his claim of having seen Jesus, and in special revelation.

Paul's testimony is that Jesus is Lord, or that the Master is Jesus. Thus, Paul asserts that he is enslaved to Christ and encourages believers to be enslaved to one another (Gal 1:10; 5:13).[16] Paul makes the confession of Jesus's Lordship (see 1 Cor 8:6), along with other Jesus-believers, as moved by the Holy Spirit (12:3). Paul joins with other believers when he quotes what may be an early Christian hymn in Phil 2:6–11. He bends the knee with all creation in confessing that Jesus is Lord (or Master).

Paul was such a powerful personality that his followers wrote letters in his name (Col, Eph, 2 Thess, 1–2 Tim, Titus). They even adopted "Paul the prisoner" as an important literary trope (Eph 3:1; Col 4:3, 10, 18). Indeed, "Paul's" sufferings are a reason for rejoicing; through them, he completes what is lacking in Christ's sufferings (1:24).

"Paul" also includes a hymn to Christ (Eph 1:15–20), celebrating that all things were created in, through, and for Christ, and that all things were reconciled through him. It is interesting to notice how often the first-person pronouns—"we" and "I"—appear in his letters. The author is "I am absent in body yet with you in spirit" (2:5). He sends brother Tychicus to the Ephesians "so that you may know how I am and what I am doing" (Eph 6:21–22; see also Titus 3:12).

The NT documents that are often referred to as the "General Epistles" also contain this insistence on testimony. The letter to the Hebrews is often considered a sermon rather than an epistle. It speaks to a pastoral problem within the audience, in which some have neglected "to meet together" (Heb 10:25). The preacher summons them to faith, putting himself and his hearers in a long line of those (mostly male) examples of faith in the Old

---

16. For counter-testimony and critical analysis of Paul's language of enslavement in Galatians, see Smith, "Hagar's Children Still Ain't Free."

Testament (11:1–38). The First Letter of John begins with testimony about what "we" have heard and seen and handled (1 John 1:1). The author says that "we testify" to life (1:2). "What we have seen and heard, we proclaim also to you so that you also might have communion with us, and our communion is with the father and with his son Jesus Messiah" (1:3). The author not only testifies to communion, but he also testifies to division. He proclaims a "last hour," as evidenced by "many antichrists" coming forth and leaving the community (2:18–19). Echoing language of the Gospel of John, the author of 1 John exhorts his readers to abide in the son and the father (2:24) and to love one another (3:11, 23–24; 4:7–12).

Things go from bad to worse in the last book of the Bible, the book of Revelation, also known as the Apocalypse of John. Witnesses die for their faith, and they become martyrs (2:10, 13; 6:9–11). Jesus, however, is the faithful witness, and he gives his testimony to John to send it to the seven churches (1:11). John was "in the spirit on the Lord's day" (1:10; see also 4:2), perhaps in prophetic ecstasy, and he heard voices and saw visions that he was to write down and send to the seven churches. The book of Revelation, then, is a book of testimony—the testimony of the martyrs, the testimony of John, and the testimony of Jesus the faithful witness. In the last chapter, Jesus speaks, "I, Jesus, sent my messenger to testify to these things to you for the assemblies," that is, for the churches (21:16) . . . . "The one who testifies to these things says, "Yes, I am coming soon" (21:20). John bears witness to Jesus, who bears witness to the things of God, as a witness to the churches. Where do you see other forms of testimony or counter-testimony in Revelation?

In the following chapters, we will give concrete examples for interpreting passages contextually, in ways that prioritize justice, and from the perspective of testimony. We begin with Luke. Smith will investigate the story of what has traditionally been called "the bent-over woman," though she calls it the story of the woman with a chronic illness that challenged her posture (Luke 13:10–17). Smith reads not only the passage but her own history and experience as the daughter of Flora Smith who suffered from a chronic illness that prevented her from stretching out her hamstrings to stand up and thus from walking.

"Textimony"

4

Centering Social Justice
in Biblical Interpretation

*The Woman with a Chronic Illness
That Challenged Her Posture (Luke 13:10–17)*

By Mitzi J. Smith

As previously mentioned, one tool that we bring to the process of interpretation, and perhaps the first, is the ability and willingness to ask questions, even uncomfortable questions that disrupt our preconceived knowledges and theological constructions. Human beings are naturally inquisitive, at least until they enter schools and other institutions where answers are provided and questioning discouraged. We are too often discouraged from raising questions or at least certain ones, particularly those for which there are no easy answers or that make some readers uncomfortable. Our uninhibited questions arise from our own experiences, epistemologies/ways of knowing (including resources for knowing or understanding), culture, interests, and so on. Thus, our questions are subjective and contextual. The word "subjective" should not be viewed negatively. It is seeing ourselves as contextual agents and subjects of reading and not simply objects of other people's readings, answers and questions. It is understanding that we do not read in isolation from the cultures, ideologies, theologies, experiences, interests, and so on that shape our human identity and impact how, why, what, and when we read or interpret. Our readings of sacred texts are not scientific, objective, or neutral, even when we claim divine inspiration. Perhaps, especially when we claim divine inspiration because only human beings need and desire it; but it does not erase or bypass our humanness, our limitations, and/or subjectivity. Or as Carolyn Sharp posits, "God's truth is beyond human comprehension and beyond the limits of human language."[1] As Brian Blount asserts, "[T]he many authoritative New Testament biblical words that sanctioned slavery (Eph 6:5; Col. 3:22; Titus 2:9; 1 Pet 2:18), devalued women (1 Cor 11; 14:34–35), or encouraged an almost blind obedience to the state (Rom 13; 1 Pet 2:13–15) are testimony to the fact that the biblical authors were themselves creatures of their contexts who, just as we do today, felt the inspiration of God and then translated the Word of God for their lives *through* those contexts."[2]

As co-authors, we share an interest and passion for social justice and biblical interpretation, but we will raise different, as well as similar questions. Our approaches and our resources for doing biblical interpretation will differ. We do not have to utilize the same approaches or resources to construct or derive legitimate and liberative meanings. Our goal is to model our distinctive and yet the sometimes overlapping or similar aspects of our approaches and resources in this chapter. We repeatedly maintain that context matters, the reader's context as well as the contexts of biblical passages (i.e., literary and historical contexts). The impact of the reader's context on interpretation begins with how we view the Bible and the selection of a pericope or Scripture passage or with the questions: Why do I want to read or what motivates me to read? What shall I read or interpret and to what end? and how shall I read?

The chapter is organized as follows: (1) discussion of the interpreter's context, reason for selecting a particular justice issue and reading approach; (2) identification of the focus passage (Luke 13:10–17) and justice framework, as well as questions that emerge; (3) translation, analysis and interrogation of the focus passage, including observations, more questions, dialogue and resources; (4) interrogation of the literary context (immediate and broader) and identification of the literary form of the passage/pericope; (5) raising questions about the historical context and some resources; and (6) finally, dialogue with secondary resources like Bible commentaries, journal articles, book chapters, and so. We are basically asking questions at every stage of the process. None of the lists of questions raised in this and

---

1. Sharp, *Wrestling the Word*, 61.
2. Brueggemann et al., *Struggling with Scripture*, 32.

succeeding chapters are exhaustive, but they serve as templates for asking questions as central to the interpretive process.

Africana Womanist Reading Approach and Context

My primary approaches to biblical interpretation are womanist and African American. This means that I privilege or prioritize the voices, experiences, history, stories, artifacts, traditions, and epistemologies of Black women (as a womanist), including my own, and the wisdom and knowledge that derives from black communities. This does not mean that I do not value those same resources in or from other communities. The term "womanist," which is a Black feminist and more, was coined by Alice Walker in her 1979 essay "Things Come Apart" and later in her book *In Search of Our Mother's Gardens* (1983). I am interested in privileging the injustices and oppressions that impacted my mother, our family, and the masses of Black women, African American communities, and humanity in general. These same injustices and oppressive polices, structures, systems, and practices contribute to the precarity of Black survival and life today. This prioritization means that the questions I raise and the concerns and challenges we have, come from my individual and communal experience as a Black woman who belongs to a larger community of Black women, men, children, and humanity.

As a Black woman raised by a Black mother confined to a wheelchair, I have been asking this question for a while now: Where are the children of the women living with disabilities in the New Testament? What happens to the children, especially the female children, when their mothers suffer from chronic illnesses? These questions lead me to the story of the woman who was bent over for eighteen years in Luke 13:10–17. These questions arise from my own subjective experiences, but I ask them also with concern for other children living with mothers with disabilities. The oppressive ways in which societies think of and treat mothers generally, particularly Black and Brown mothers suffering from chronic illnesses or debilitating addictions drive my initial questions and impact what passage I choose to interpret. I remember my mother telling me that at the beginning of her confinement to the wheelchair, neighbors attempted to encourage her to surrender her children to Franklin Village. In the 1960s Franklin Village in Columbus, Ohio was re-tasked with providing foster care and institutional services for abused and neglected children. My mother (or father) neither abused nor neglected us, but society tends to view mothers with disabilities as ill-equipped because of any visible or assumed physical or mental limitations.

Raising More Questions and Making Observations: The Justice Framework

As we focus on Luke 13:10–17 with my initial questions in mind, I raise other questions. Questions can be more important than answers. I ask additional questions not with the intention of answering them all, but as part of the process of engagement and dialogue between me, as subjective reader, and the biblical text and its contexts, and between the broader justice issue of mothers suffering with chronic illnesses and Luke 13:10–17. Remember, interpretation or meaning making is the process of negotiation between the reader (and her context) and the biblical (con)text. Some of my questions will be about the justice framework or lens that I place in conversation with Luke 13:10–17. Other questions will concern the passage under consideration, namely its specific language (including patterns and repetitions), rhetoric, and narrative (including characterization), its literary context, and its historical context. The following are questions that arise from the justice framework I selected:

1. How does a mother's (or father's) chronic illness impact her children and her as a mother and woman?

2. How do individuals and communities, including churches, react to mothers suffering from chronic illnesses?

3. In my experience and in our communities, when are children removed from homes of mothers with chronic illnesses or addictions?

4. What happens to the children who are removed from homes where their mothers suffer from chronic illnesses or addictions?

5. From what types of chronic illnesses do mothers suffer most?

6. How often are children of mothers suffering from chronic illnesses rendered homeless or exposed?

7. Are Black mothers disproportionately impacted and how or why?

8. Are race, class, gender, and sexuality factors? If so, how?

9. How is a person living with a disability impacted socially and sexually?

10. How is a person living with a disability silenced, treated as invisible, and/or dehumanized?

11. What are some of the things that other people do to persons living with disabilities that they don't do to other people?

12. What help is available to mothers suffering from chronic illnesses and/or addictions in general and/or their children?

13. How does the church help and/or further oppress mothers (and fathers) suffering from chronic illnesses and their children?

In addition to drawing from personal experience or commitments, students should perform some preliminary research of reliable resources, including national statistics and online articles from creditable news outlets, on the topic. For example, in this case the Center for Disease Control (CDC) provides statistics for chronic diseases in America including a "Chronic Diseases Fact Sheet" at https://www.cdc.gov/chronicdisease/resources/infographic/chronic-diseases.htm and https://www.cdc.gov/chronicdisease/resources/publications/fact-sheets.htm. The Children's Bureau of the US Department of Health and Human Services provides information about reunification of children with parents who suffer from behavior and physical health challenges: https://www.childwelfare.gov/topics/permanency/reunification/disability/. Students should read other resources before and during their examination of the biblical text. They will encourage other questions and encourage critical thinking and creativity. These other resources include monographs, as well as journal articles. This research does not mean students must read entire books in the limited time allotted them. Students can read several book reviews, for example, to determine if the book or particular chapters will be helpful (or how helpful). See, for example, the following texts:

Brown, Maxine Childress. *On the Beat of Truth: A Hearing Daughter's Stories of Her Black Deaf Parents*. Washington, DC: Gallaudet University Press, 2013.

Connor, David J., et al. *DisCrit—Disability Studies and Critical Race Theory in Education*. New York: Teacher's College, 2016.

Filax, Gloria. *Disabled Mothers: Stories and Scholarship by and About Mothers with Disabilities*. Bradford, ON: Demeter, 2014.

Gallop, Jane. *Sexuality, Disability, and Aging: Queer Temporalities of the Phallus*. Durham, NC: Duke University Press, 2019.

Mason, Mary Grimley, and Linda Long-Bellil. *Taking Care: Lessons from Mothers with Disabilities*. Lanham, MD: University Press of America, 2012.

Valle, Jan W., and David J. Connor. *Rethinking Disability: A Disability Studies Approach to Inclusive Practices*. 2nd ed. New York: Routledge, 2019.

As stated, engagement with the above and other resources will result in more questions as well as provide creative and significance ways of constructing dialogue between the contemporary justice issue and interpretation of the biblical passage and its context. This is different from dialogue with biblical commentators, our final step in the process, as mentioned below. Students should never presume that starting with a justice framework eliminates the necessity of doing the other labor of close reading of the language and literary and historical contexts of the passage under consideration.

Translating, Analyzing, and Interrogating the Pericope/Passage (Luke 13:10–17)

If students have studied Greek, this is an opportunity for students to practice their language skills. Translating the passage familiarizes the interpreter with some linguistic patterns, grammar, semantics, and so on that can only be detected in the ancient language. Readers who cannot or do not translate the Greek or Hebrew for themselves, are relying on the translations, which are interpretations, of others (In fact, the Greek Testament is an interpretation). It matters who translates. I repeat, *it matters who translates*. Context matters even at the level of translation of the ancient language. Every translator (interpreter) brings their own presuppositions to the task of translation; it is also an act of interpretation. Each reader's context is both like other readers and distinct. Embrace and trust your capacity to see and interpret differently. My English translation of Luke 13:10–17 is as follows:

> [10]Jesus was teaching in one of the synagogues during the Sabbath, [11]and witness! (ἰδοὺ) the existence of a woman with a spirit (πνεῦμα) that made her ill (ἀσθενείας) for eighteen years; her back was bent over (συγκύπτουσα) and she was unable to straighten up

(ἀνακύψαι) to any degree. ¹²When Jesus *saw* her, he called her to himself and said, "Woman, you have been released (ἀπολέλυσαι) from your illness (ἀσθενείας σου)." ¹³He placed his hands on her and immediately she straightened up perfectly (ἀνωρθώθη) and glorified God. ¹⁴But, upset that Jesus healed her during the Sabbath, the head of the synagogue responded and said to the crowd, "There are six days during which you must work; therefore, during those days, come to experience healing, but not on the Sabbath day." ¹⁵But the Lord replied to him and said, "Hypocrite! Don't each of you release his ox or donkey from the stall and lead it to drink water during the Sabbath? ¹⁶ But this is a daughter of Abraham, which, witness! (ἰδού), the Adversary (ὁ σατανᾶς) imprisoned for eighteen years. Wasn't it necessary that she be released (λυθῆναι) from this confinement on the Sabbath day?" ¹⁷And when Jesus said these things, all his opponents were humiliated. But the entire crowd rejoiced at all the extraordinary things that had occurred through him.

Luke's Gospel provides his readers with a testimony about Jesus's encounter with the woman who had a chronic illness that challenged her body so that she could not straighten her back but appeared folded over. The text invites readers to become witnesses. Twice we are invited to see or witness this woman, her condition, and confinement, through the narrator and through Jesus's direct speech (vv. 10, 16). Consequently, the ancient audience and contemporary readers are witnesses—physically and historically distant from each other and from the event, of course—of the woman's condition and the encounter between her and Jesus that culminates with her healing. One might make a distinction between the witness as testifier and the witness as observer; often the observer becomes the testifier. Thus, I translate the Greek verb ἰδού (second-person aorist imperative middle of εἶδον) as *witness!*, as in bear witness. At strategic points in the retelling of the story, Jesus commands the synagogue attendees to see, acknowledge, and/or affirm his testimony. Witnesses testify, which is perhaps what they do at verse 17b: They cheered at the extraordinary sight. We can see or witness what is in the text (world of the text) and what is in front of the text, neither of which is ever an objective seeing or witnessing. Twice at the beginning of the healing story and at the end, Jesus directs the audience to witness (with the Greek verb ἰδού) the woman's chronic condition and how she was imprisoned (but is now free).

Readers must be willing to sit with the biblical passage, over time—to read and reread it as if reading it for the first time, without assuming they already know what "it says" or should say. Texts do not say, just as words, as symbols, don't speak; they are read or interpreted. As children we learned the three R's which are *Reading, 'Riting and 'Rithmetic*, but in our book the triple R's could be Reading, Rereading, and Repeat (or re-reading as many times as context and time allows).

We must allow ourselves to witness what we have not previously noticed, to re/create our own interpretative testimony. Start with noting the obvious or what seems immediately apparent (e.g., who are the characters?). The more time you spend noticing words, phrases, syntax (how words are arranged or fit together), patterns, repetitions, sequence, the strange, the (un)expected, and so forth, the more you will see. The justice or contemporary lens will/should also provoke some questions, comparisons, and observations that might otherwise go unnoticed and not voiced.

Observations, Questions, and Dialogue

1. The woman is anonymous. Why is she anonymous? What is the impact of her anonymity?

2. Why is it more important to the story that she is a daughter of Abraham—her relationship to an ancestor and/or community—rather than her individual identity? Shouldn't both be significant?

3. It is interesting that she is described as a "daughter" but there is no mention of her own family or children. Perhaps her illness prevented her from getting married and birthing children.

4. She arrives at the synagogue alone.

5. She is described as having a spirit (πνεῦμα) that impacted the range of motion of her back or caused deterioration of her muscles for eighteen years (13:11).

6. What is meant by "a spirit"? Should we presume the spirit is evil, rather than good or neither and why?

7. Jesus summons the woman and then heals her, almost as if the healing is an exhibition and her body is the exhibit.

8. The woman is silent; she is asked nothing and says nothing.

9. The controversy is among men and the woman's body is at the center of it.

10. Jesus puts his hands on her body without her permission. Could this be a problem in the text and/or in our modern context?

11. How do we, especially women and children, make exceptions for people with authority and power when it comes to allowing others to touch our bodies without our permission? When and how has or can making such exceptions lead to abuse?

12. Jesus compares what he did for the woman on the Sabbath with what is done for animals on the Sabbath. How might this be a problematic comparison?

13. Is this the first time she is seen or noticed by anyone in the synagogue and if so, what are the implications? It seems she had been rendered invisible and her condition and presence normalized by the synagogue leader and regular attendees.

14. Because she was bent over and unable to look up, she did not see Jesus. Perhaps, she relied on being seen and not overlooked [like my mother and many disabled persons].

15. The synagogue leader is also anonymous. What is the possible significance of his anonymity? How is his anonymity mitigated by his position and gender? How is the impact of his anonymity different from the woman's?

16. The synagogue leader does not address the woman before or after her healing. After the healing, the synagogue leader turns to the crowd and addresses them. He is more concerned with persuading the crowd to agree with his opposition to the healing on the Sabbath than with the restoration of the woman. What does he gain from his opposition? What does he risk?

17. How old or young might she have been when "a spirit" of illness challenged her posture?

18. How might you name this woman so as to empower her?

19. Jesus addresses this woman.

20. There is no mention of faith in this story. I state this because too often students impose faith in healing stories in the gospels. Healing and miracles were not uncommon in ancient cultures.

21. When Jesus places his hands on the woman, she straightens up.

22. Jesus set the woman free from the spirit that caused her illness because he could and it was the just thing to do, on the Sabbath or on any day of the week.

23. What systems, people, or ideologies/theologies do you think may have prevented others from setting this woman free from her illness? Perhaps the woman's only opportunity to be present among people who might heal or help her was on the Sabbath in the synagogue. But the ideo-theology of some, including of the religious leaders, did not support or make room for such a healing on the Sabbath in that synagogue.

24. Jesus sums up the woman's predicament with the words "the Adversary imprisoned her." What does that mean?

25. This woman is caught in the middle of hostilities among men. Her story takes place in the middle of conflict.

26. Jesus calls the leaders of the synagogues and others who oppose the woman's healing "hypocrites" because they will take care of their animals on the Sabbath but not a chronically ill woman. Women, chronically sick women, are treated not even like the animals; they are valued less.

27. Why do you think it matters that she is a daughter of Abraham and what is the significance? How might calling the woman a daughter of Abraham erase her own familial context?

28. Jews and gentiles visited synagogues.

29. What verbs occur most often in the pericope and what do you think is the significance?

30. What other repetitions do you notice?

These are just a few observations that we can state and questions we can raise about this story.

My mother was once diagnosed as having degenerative arthritis. That diagnosis was abandoned when it did not coincide with her long-term physical condition. She did not have the same degree of joint deterioration in her hands, for example. But over the years, without proper health care and lack of adequate insurance—insurance that did not pay for long term therapy—her condition deteriorated. Her leg joints stiffened and locked at a ninety-degree angle and eventually her back weakened. Similar to the woman in Luke, she could not straighten up. But my mother, unlike the woman in Luke, could no longer walk. My mother attended church every Sabbath as a Seventh-Day Adventist (SDA). Even when she felt badly, she insisted we help get her ready for church. At one time in her life, my mother drove a car with hand controls, but most often she depended either on one of her children or a church member to transport her to church. However, my mother did not meet a healer in the church, even though I never once witnessed or heard her express one word of unbelief. In fact, it was a long time before the church built a ramp for the physically disabled to enter and exit the church without fear of being dropped or of the scrapes or bruises caused by careless and/or inexperienced persons handling their wheelchairs.

My mother grew up in a (Methodist Episcopal) Christian household (raised by her grandparents after her mother died of pneumonia) that read the Bible daily and attended church weekly. My mother had strong faith and seldom, if ever, expressed hopelessness. She joined the SDA church when two women Bible workers came to visit her—Sisters Martin and Clark (both deceased)—and not because she needed Bible studies; I think she was also lonely. What blessed my mother most was that Sisters Martin and Clark did not come simply with their Bible studies. Those church ladies saw that my mother had small children, and so they took her dirty laundry with them when they left. And when they returned, they brought her clean clothes *and* their Bible studies. That's why my mother joined the SDA church. I joined because she did. Churches often teach that if one has enough faith (as little as a mustard seed), then one could be healed. If a person is not healed, it is the believer's fault or shortcoming.

The following are some questions that my experience growing up with my mother who was unable to walk and had to survive within a church, society and systems that generally did not care or plan for her—my contemporary (in)justice lens—prompt these further questions:

1. What might be the impact of the woman's diagnosis (spirit of weakness or deterioration) or of religio-cultural beliefs about the origins of illness on the woman in Luke? How might she be (mis)treated in the synagogue, at home, and/or in society because of those beliefs and her diagnosis?

2. If the woman had children, what might have happened to them given her chronic condition?

3. What is the impact of chronic illness on a woman's ability to survive, on her social class?

4. How did this woman survive? What difference does gender, class, ethnicity/race, religion, and age make?

5. What social, religious, or political systems negatively or positively impact her (in)ability to survive and experience quality of life?

6. What kind of medical treatment might this woman have had access to?

7. How might Jesus's treatment of the woman help us think more progressively about contemporary health care?

8. When is our theology an obstacle to compassion and healthfulness? When does it contribute to debilitating dis-ease?

9. What do you think attending synagogue each week did for this woman?

In my mother's case, the Adversary was a society that did not pay a living wage and an inadequate and inhumane health care system. When my mother could not afford bus fare (and miracles were far and few between—though she experienced some like the wind landing a bus ticket in front of her frozen feet at the bus stop, as I mentioned earlier), she often walked miles to work, in the dead of winter and heat of summer, for low wages. When she could no longer work, she relied on Medicaid that gave her access to doctors who changed frequently and who seldom, if ever, remembered or knew her name or her medical history. When my siblings and I accompanied her to appointments, the doctors asked the same questions (few showed compassion; many made us angry, even as children) and were seldom helpful. My mother just loved getting out of the house. If she luckily landed an intern or doctor who halfway cared for her as a human being, she would talk fondly of him and his mannerisms. Medicaid would not pay for the long-term therapy my mother needed. When it did pay for therapy and the therapists put my mother in the water, she could stand up straight and walk through the water—her temporary miracle. It fed her hope. It seemed whenever she began making progress, her Medicaid benefits expired.

Examining and Interrogating the Literary Context— Luke's Gospel

The literary context is the entire Gospel of Luke. We make observations and raise questions of the pericope's relationship to the broader context of Luke's gospel, including the episodes that *immediately precede* and *immediately follow the story*, which is the immediate literary context.

Compare Similar Stories

What stories are similar to our story that permit us to compare them. I identify this passage as a Sabbath healing story of a woman that provokes opposition or conflict. The healing takes place in the synagogue, and the synagogue leader opposes the healing because it is done on the Sabbath. The synagogue leader attempts to arouse the crowds, but they and their fellow opponents are shamed when Jesus exposes their hypocrisy (13:14–17). Some readers will classify this as an exorcism story because of the mention of "spirit" (πνεῦμα) as the cause of the woman's condition (13:11a). But does this story follow the pattern of "exorcism" stories in Luke?

Jesus's first miracle in Luke is the exorcism in the synagogue on the Sabbath. Jesus is also teaching when a man having a spirit of an unclean demon (πνεῦμα δαιμονίου ἀκαθάρτου, 4:33; cf. 6:18, 7:21; 8:2, 29) is present. In that episode the unclean spirit addresses Jesus, requests that Jesus leave *them* alone, and identifies him. Jesus rebukes the unclean spirit, silences him, and commands him to exit the man's body. The crowd is amazed, but nobody expresses opposition to the healing on the Sabbath (4:31–37). We find the same pattern in the summary of Jesus's exorcism activities at 4:41: Unclean spirit(s)/demons shout at Jesus; they identify him; Jesus rebukes and silences the unclean spirit(s); and Jesus commands the unclean spirit(s) to exit the man's body. This story appears in what is considered by many scholars as the earliest canonical gospel of Mark (1:21–28; Luke 4:31–37); Luke found it useful for his narrative, it appears (according to the two-source hypothesis that Luke and Matthew borrowed material from Mark and a hypothetical sayings source called Q). Unlike the story of the woman who could not fully extent her back when she stood up, we find both the nouns spirit and demon (δαιμονία) to describe his condition or what possesses him. We should not be quick to see every illness as the result of an evil spirit or as demonic. Jesus does not touch the man, but he touches the woman in our text. Those who witness the scene of the man's exorcism raise no objection to it happening on the Sabbath, but they are astonished at Jesus's authority before and after the exorcism. If this pattern for exorcisms holds, in general, throughout Luke's Gospel, the woman who cannot fully extend her back may not be an object of exorcism in the sense of release from demons inhabiting her body (cf. 5:12–16).

Since our story does not follow the above pattern of a typical Lukan (or Gospel) exorcism story, I view our focus pericope as *a story about the healing of an anonymous woman with a chronic illness in the synagogue on the Sabbath that provokes opposition.* Are there any similar stories in Luke? The story of the man with the distorted right hand is like our story (6:6–11). There Jesus is also teaching in the synagogue on the Sabbath; Jesus calls to the man (who also does not approach, or ask, Jesus for healing), tells him to stretch out his hand, and he is healed when he conforms. Different from our story, Jesus intentionally defies the scribes and Pharisees who are opposed to Jesus feeding his disciples or healing on the Sabbath (6:15). Jesus demonstrates that it is lawful to do good and save life on the Sabbath (6:1–11). Also, unlike our story, the healing narrative of the man "with the withered hand" precedes the opposition to feeding on the Sabbath. But the story of the woman whose posture is challenged and the man with the distorted hand address opposition to Jesus healing on the Sabbath. In the end, both stories are about one man, Jesus. Both the woman in our text and the man with the distorted right hand are anonymous and do not seek healing. Perhaps, they had not expected to find healing in the synagogue because of the many years that had passed without finding restoration in that space; they had become accustomed to being ignored when entering the synagogue and leaving in the same condition. Are we witnessing a sort of internalization of normalized apathy and impotence among the synagogue attendees?

The condition of the man with the distorted hand, however, is not attributed to a spirit; perhaps this is because it was known what caused it or his condition was diagnosable. Is there anyone else described as having a spirit of (deteriorating) illness in Luke? The spirit that has rendered the woman unable to fully extend her back muscles is not described as unclean. Perhaps the phrase "spirit of illness or weakness" is a way of saying that her condition could not be diagnosed. Perhaps, the phrase "spirit of deteriorating illness" signifies that nobody understood the cause of her illness; it must be a "spirit." Unlike the man possessed with an unclean spirit, but like the man with the distorted hand, Jesus sees the woman and calls her to himself (as opposed to avoiding or silencing her). Jesus asks her if she would like to be set free from the cause of her illness and thereby the illness itself (13:11–12). She is given a choice, but the unclean spirits in other texts have no choice; they must evacuate the bodies they occupy. When Jesus lays his hands on the woman, her deteriorating body is immediately restored (13:13a). Jesus does not lay hands on any person with an "unclean spirit" while healing her, him or them in Luke. After her healing, the woman whose posture had been challenged for eighteen years praises God [not Jesus] (13:13b). When do other women praise God in Luke? When do others who are healed praise God in Luke? How are women in need of healing depicted in Luke and how often are they alone and without help, especially compared to men who suffer from illnesses?

Immediate Literary Context of Luke 13:10–17

The cohesive episode (or verses) that precedes the passage we are interpreting is the so-called "parable of the barren fig tree" (13:6–9); the "parable of the mustard seed" follows our pericope (13:18–19). I say so-called because we must be careful with allowing captions in Bibles to restrict or govern how we should interpret a passage or pericope.

Here are a few observations I have while examining the immediate literary context (13:6–9, 18–19) in relation to our passage (13:10–17):

1. In all three episodes (13:6–9, 10–17, and 18–19) Jesus is teaching.

2. The parables of the fig tree and mustard seed frame the story of the woman healed in our story. How do they both point to her as well as beyond her?

3. At the center of both parables is a tree—a fig tree and a mustard tree. The former withered or shrunk (which is what can happen as people age and cannot stand up straight due to bone loss or other problems) like the woman before she is healed, and the latter stands tall like the woman after Jesus heals her.

4. The parable of the withered fig tree demonstrates how the Israelite people must repent or perish (13:5). The woman whose body is challenged by a chronic disease is a "daughter of Abraham" or an Israelite (13:16). She may be more important, unfortunately, for what she represents than as an individual.

5. The parables that precede and follow the healing of the woman demonstrate the long-term care or attention that people will/should provide a plant so that it grows into a fruitful tree, giving it a chance to grow straight and tall for years. The story of the woman whose back has folded over demonstrates how disabilities become chronic from years of neglect by society and church [and other religious communities] and how persons suffering like this woman can be restored to a condition before her illness when we stop, see/witness, and act in powerful ways.

The Broader Lukan Literary Context

Again, the broader literary context of Luke 13:10–17 is the Gospel of Luke. The pericope must be interpreted within the literary context of Luke's Gospel *before moving beyond Luke to other Gospels for purposes of comparison.* We can observe and analyze at the level of words, phrases, or other language units. We can compare healing episodes involving women or women and conflict, for example, as done above when we identified the literary form. We will examine other episodes of women and the use of words like *spirit* and *adversary* in Luke and what light they might shed on our passage.

> At this point, Newheart reminds us that it's probably good to read through the Gospel of Luke. Yes, the whole Gospel! It's not that long—only fifty pages in the *New Oxford Annotated Bible*! And if you're an overachiever, you can read the Acts of the Apostles, which is about the same length as Luke. Acts, of course, is Luke's second volume.

1. Are other women healed in the synagogue in Luke and if so, how do those episodes compare to our story? If not, who is primarily healed in synagogues in Luke? What is the significance?

2. How does the healing of this woman fit with Jesus's mission or purpose in Luke? For example, do we find connections between our pericope and Luke 4:18?

3. Are other women's dis-eased bodies at the center of male controversy in Luke? If so, what are the implications?

4. How are women in need of healing depicted in Luke and how often are they alone and without help, especially compared to men who suffer from illnesses?

5. This woman does not speak before, during or after her encounter with Jesus. Is this a pattern in Luke or not? What significance might we draw, or so what?

6. Are there other occurrences of the phrase "spirit of illness" in Luke, or is this a Lucan *hapax legomenon* (a unique or only occurrence)? What significance might we draw or so what?

7. How are Jesus's word and actions in this pericope typical or atypical of his depiction elsewhere in Luke? What significance might we draw, or so what?

8. When and why does Luke's Gospel evoke the term "the Satan" elsewhere, and how is our pericope similar and/or different from those other instances? What meaning do we derive from the collective occurrences? How is the use of the term distinct or similar in our passage to other occurrences? What significance might we draw, or so what?

9. Upon whom else does Jesus place his hands or touch persons's bodies when healing them? So what?

10. When or how often is the length of illness or age of women, as opposed to men or children, revealed?

11. What connections can we make between the number of years that the woman suffered and other numbers mentioned in the pericope and in the immediate literary context?

12. It appears that healing, even from barrenness in Elizabeth's case and humiliation in Mary's situation, is evidence that God has looked favorably on God's people (e.g., 1:25, 48; 7:16).

13. When we compare the language of seeing in our story with similar language in the birth narratives, what theological point might Luke be making in our text?

14. Where do we find the Satan/Adversary elsewhere in Luke? What evidence might we find that resists always equating the Satan/Adversary with an (evil) spirit? In what way does the Satan/Adversary seem immortal (or not) in Luke?

15. How does the Satan/Adversary represent anything or anyone that diminishes human wholeness and freedom of movement or of quality of life in Luke (cf. Job 2:1–8)?

16. Where do we find other healing stories in Luke where the word *faith* is not mentioned or *faith* is not a factor? So what?

These questions represent some of the ways we can read our text in the larger literary context of Luke's Gospel. For example, in response to number eleven above, it is interesting that in the parable of the fig tree (the preceding literary context, 13:6–9) the owner of a vineyard who planted a fig tree observed for three years that the tree was fruitless. In our text, the synagogue leader insists that work, including healing, must be done during the six days of the week and not on the Sabbath (13:14). Three years multiplied by six days equals eighteen. The woman suffered for eighteen years. The question the interpreter must always ask is *so what*? Sometimes, we will not be able to answer the *so what* question, but it is just as significant to raise the question.

It may be significant that Jesus touches the woman in our text. Question 9 above asks who does Jesus lay hands on or touch and not touch when he performs a healing or exorcism in Luke ? In the healing of the man with the withered hand, which also occurs on the Sabbath, provoking controversy from some scribes and Pharisees, Jesus does not touch him (6:6–11). Similarly, the Lukan Jesus does not touch men while he performs exorcisms (4:31–37; 8:26–39; 9:37–43). Does Jesus primarily touch women he heals? Perhaps, Jesus does primarily touch the women he cures (or they touch him); see Luke 7:30–49; 8:40–56 (Jairus' daughter and woman suffering from chronic bleeding); 13:10–17 (woman with deteriorating back muscles); contra, Simon's mother-in-law, 4:38–39.

Partially in response to question 14 above, I offer the following: On a particular day the woman whose illness impacts her posture encounters Jesus as someone willing and able to heal her in the synagogue. If their property—an ox or donkey—needed to be rescued, the day of the week would not matter. She has come to the synagogue for eighteen long years where she had been treated as less than their animals. Is there a literary, semantic, and theological relationship between all who oppose Jesus and the Adversary/Satan (ὁ σατανᾶς) that limited the range of movement of the woman's body, refusing to release her? Are the spirit of a degenerative illness that inflicted her *and* the adversary that imprisoned her, making her condition chronic, necessarily one and the same or interconnected? When the seventy return from fulfilling their house-to-house mission to cure the sick and proclaim the good news, they report to Jesus with joy that even demons submitted to them (10:17). To this report, Jesus replies that "I had witnessed the *Adversary*, like a star, fall from the heaven" (my translation) (10:18; cf. Job 1:6–12). This translation could mean that the *Adversary/Satan* fell from heaven before the seventy went out. If we translate the verse as "I have witnessed the *Adversary*, like a star, fall from heaven," we might conclude that the success of the seventy engenders or contributes to the *Adversary's* defeat. In what way is Jesus speaking metaphorically? Literally? Does the fall of the *Adversary* refer to the overcoming of any illness, rejection of good news, or bodily possession that is against wholeness, health, and good news? Are *adversaries* and/or adversative people and powers defeated anytime people are cured, healed, or made whole? Is *the Adversary* symbolic of spirits, human beings, or institutions that opposes or challenge the curative and holistic work of God?

We can raise many questions of the broader literary context to help interpret our passage, but we will only attempt to respond to one or a few at a time. And our responses can change depending on our approach and/or the interpretative lens or framework through or with which we read biblical passages.

Historical Context

Remember that biblical texts, as ancient or historical documents, can also contribute to historical context. The OT often provides historical context for NT texts. Students might raise many questions but choose one to three historical questions to address in the interpretation paper. We raise the following questions of the historical context:

1. What can we know about the children of women with chronic and/or fatal illnesses in the first century? What happened to them?

2. What kind of medical treatment was available to women with chronic illnesses in the first century?

3. What can we know about the kind of medical care men and women received and how it may have been gendered? What can we know about the medical treatment poor people received versus the wealthy, and for what ailments?

4. What can we discover about the connection between poverty, gender, and chronic illness in the historical context?

5. How did the ancients understand demons and spirits?

6. Did ancient people in Judea and the surrounding regions or in the broader Roman Empire connect a created or lesser spirit being or deity to illnesses, especially unexplained illnesses and if so, how?

7. What can we know about "the Satan" in other ancient literature? Ryan Stokes traces the chronological evolution of the portrayal of figures connected with the concept of a "satan." He concludes that, over time, the literature transformed a one-time agent of YHWH into God's principal enemy.[3]

Here are a few resources for exploring these historical questions:

Bazzana, Giovanni B. *Having the Spirit of Christ: Spirit Possession and Exorcism In Early Christ Groups.* New Haven, CT: Yale University Press, 2020.

Bendick, Jeanne. *Galen and the Gateway to Medicine.* San Francisco: Ignatius, 2002.

Cotter, Wendy. *Miracles in Greco-Roman Antiquity: A Sourcebook.* New York: Routledge, 1999.

Green, Joel B., et al., eds. *Dictionary of Jesus and the Gospels.* 2nd ed. Downers Grove, IL: InterVarsity, 2013.

Nutton, Vivian. *Ancient Medicine.* 2nd ed. New York: Routledge, 2012.

Stokes, Ryan E. *The Satan: How God's Executioner Became the Enemy.* Grand Rapids: Eerdmans, 2019.

Dialogue with Biblical Commentators and Other Scholarly Works

We *strongly discourage* students from reading biblical commentaries, monographs or other secondary literature that provide scholarly commentary of the passage under consideration (except perhaps dictionaries) until they have critically examined the pericope themselves and/in its literary

---

3. Stokes, *Satan.*

context. Readers have become accustomed to surrendering their interpretative agency to scholars. Often, readers can arrive at many of the same conclusions found in secondary literature or scholarly works if they sit with the text, reading it closely and critically in its literary context. *Only after* students have followed the above steps should they read commentaries and other scholarly works that interpret the pericope. In this final stage of interpretation, the commentaries that students engage or dialogue with should be diverse in terms of race, ethnicity, gender, sexuality, interpretative approaches and so forth.

Unless we surrender our agency, experience, contexts and so on to others—to the extent that we can—we each bring something unique to the task of interpretation. If we relinquish our interpretative agency, we bring someone else's voice, contexts, experiences, ideologies, theologies, and priorities to the reading of texts. We all bring our own experiences, presuppositions, and contexts to the task of interpretation. Our presuppositions (good, bad, neutral or a combination), contexts, and experiences allow us to see differently and sometimes what others do not or cannot see or imagine. But as human beings, as flesh and blood readers, we also arrive at the task of interpretation with limitations precisely because of our humanness and our uniqueness.

Below are a few select commentaries and other secondary sources that might be helpful to engage in dialogue with the work you have already done with the text. The following is a brief select list of recommended commentaries and monographs for our focus pericope. Students should by no means neglect to search for relevant book chapters and/or journal articles as well. Strive for a balance of writers in terms of race, gender, ethnicity, sexual orientation, and so on.

Select Commentaries and Monographs

Bovon, François, and Helmut Koester. *Luke 2: A Commentary of the Gospel of Luke 9:51–19:27.* Hermeneia. Minneapoli: Fortress, 2013.

Brawley, Robert A. "Luke." *Fortress Commentary on the Bible: The New Testament,* edited by Margaret Aymer et al., 217–63. Minneapolis: Fortress, 2014.

Crowder, Stephanie Buckhanon. "Gospel of Luke." *True to Our Native Land: An African American Commentary of the New Testament.* Minneapolis: Fortress, 2007.

Fox, Bethany McKinney, and John Swinton. *Disability and the Way of Jesus: Holistic Healing in the Gospels and the Church.* Downers Grove, IL: InterVarsity, 2019.

Henning, Meghan R. *Hell Hath No Fury: Gender, Disability, and the Invention of Damned Bodies in Early Christian Literature.* New Haven, CT: Yale University Press, 2021.

Melcher, Sarah J., et al. *The Bible and Disability: A Commentary.* Waco, TX: Baylor University Press, 2017.

Moss, Candida. *Divine Bodies: Resurrecting Perfection in the New Testament and Early Christianity.* New Haven, CT: Yale University Press, 2019.

———. *Plagues of God: How Disease Shaped Religious Faith.* New York: HarperOne, 2021.

Reid, Barbara, and Shelly Matthews. *Luke 10–24.* Wisdom Commentary Series. Collegeville, MN: Liturgical, 2021.

Solevag, Anna Rebecca. *Negotiating the Disabled Body: Representations of Disability in Early Christian Texts.* Atlanta: Society of Biblical Literature, 2018.

Tupamahu, Ekaputra. "The Gospel of Luke." *An Asian Introduction to the New Testament,* edited by Johnson Thomaskutty, 103–26. Minneapolis: Fortress, 2022.

5

Jesus the Truth-Testifier on Automatic Pilate

(John 18:33–38)

By Michael Newheart

WE NOW TURN TO the Gospel of John, a book in which the concept of witness or testifying plays an important role. Specifically, we look at John 18:33–38, a scene in the trial before Pilate (18:28—19:16a), in which Jesus's work of testifying plays a major role. This passage was the Gospel reading for the twenty-ninth Sunday after Pentecost in Year B, which most recently was November 21, 2021. I was serving as bridge pastor at First Congregational Church (UCC) in West Hartford, Connecticut, a post that I served until February 6, 2022.[1] I preached on this passage to "kill two birds with one stone" (to use a violent image; actually, no creatures were harmed in this sermon, at least not to my knowledge), that is, to proclaim the word but also to get something done on the book. My interests in this passage were pastoral; I used it to build up people's faith. Yet my interests were also academic in that I wrote a PhD dissertation on John, which was published, and I have written an additional book on John. Indeed, I even

---

1. A bridge pastor serves between the interim pastor and the settled pastor. At this writing (July 25, 2022), I am interim pastor of Second Baptist Church, Suffield, Connecticut. This interim will soon conclude, and I will assume on August 28, 2022, the interim pastorate of First Baptist Church, East Greenwich, Rhode Island.

devoted a chapter of that latter book to the trial before Pilate. I am eager to dig into it again.

I will begin with this scene from the trial before Pilate. I have set it on the page in poetic form so that you might see the various rhythms of the text. The translation is the NSV, Newheart Slanted Version (!). Seriously, the translation is my own.

> [33]And again, Pilate came into the praetorium
> and called Jesus and said to him,
> "Are you the king of the Jews?"
> [34]Jesus said,
> "Is this your own idea,
> or has someone said this about me?"
> [35]Pilate said,
> "I'm not a Jew, am I?
> Your nation and your high priests have turned you over to me.
> What have you done?"
> [36]Jesus said,
> "My reign is not from this world.
> If my reign were from this world,
> my henchmen would have rescued me,
> so that I wouldn't have been handed over to the Jews.
> But my reign is not from here."
> [37]Then Pilate said to him,
> "Then you are a king?"
> Jesus answered,
> "You say that I'm a king.
> I have been born for this,
> and I've come into the world for this:
> that I might testify to the truth.
> Everyone who hears my voice is of the truth."
> [38]Pilate says to him,
> "What's truth?"

Now I raise the following questions about the text:

∗ How does the presentation of Jesus's trial before Pilate in John compare to the presentation in the other three Gospels? How is Jesus depicted? How is Pilate depicted? Why the difference between the representation in John and the other three Gospels?

* Why might Pilate have thought that Jesus was "king of the Jews"? In what sense does Jesus answer yes to Pilate's question? In what sense does he answer no?

* In what sense is Pilate depicted as a sympathetic character? In what sense is he not?

* Flip through the Gospel. Give particular attention to chapters 18 and 19. How is Jesus depicted in these chapters? How is Pilate?

* If Jesus's reign is not from this world, where is it from?

* Use a concordance to find where else in the Gospel the word "truth" appears. What is the answer to Pilate's question, "What's truth?" In what ways has Jesus testified to the truth?

* What connections might there be between 18:37, "Everyone who hears my voice is of the truth," and 10:1–18, the so-called Good Shepherd Discourse?

The Trial in Its Literary Context

Immediately prior to this episode, the "trial before Pilate" begins (18:28–32). They—that is, the Jews (18:31b)—take Jesus from the high priest Caiaphas to the praetorium, which is Pilate's headquarters. This is the first episode in the trial. John gives us a temporal marker: "It was early in the morning" (18:28b). He also lets us inside the heads of Jesus's "takers," who don't enter the praetorium so that they can eat the Passover. There is a certain irony that they have no qualms about killing a man, but they are meticulous in following the law to participate in their ritual meal. Pilate speaks with the Jews twice, and they answer him twice. He asks them about the charge they bring against Jesus. They really don't answer—in this Gospel, characters, especially Jesus, have difficulty giving straight answers—and they simply say that Jesus is a criminal. Pilate tells the Jews to judge Jesus by their law, but they—that is, the Jews, John says—are not able to execute anyone. Then John says that the Jews's statement indicates that Jesus's death would fulfill what he had earlier said. Indeed, this statement—one might say, this Gospel—only makes sense on this side of Jesus's crucifixion. Three times Jesus speaks of himself or the Human One (Son of Man) being lifted up (3:14; 8:28; 12:32–33). Since we know that Jesus died by crucifixion, all this resonates. Otherwise, it's confusing. Jesus as the Human One is lifted up in crucifixion by the Romans and in exaltation by God.

After our passage, in which Pilate speaks to Jesus, he speaks again to the Jews (18:38b–40). Pilate says that he doesn't have a case against Jesus. OK, Mr. Procurator Person, you don't have a case, then release him! It's not that simple. Pilate speaks about a Passover custom whereby he releases someone—out of the goodness of his heart, right? So, how 'bout the passionate Pilate proposes that he release the King of the Jews. (But didn't Jesus just reject that title?) The Jews, however, demonstrate that he is not their king by saying that they want Barabbas, who was a bandit, that is, a political revolutionary (18:40). "Barabbas" literally "son of the father," so this is the one they want, not Jesus, who is the true Son of the Father.

The trial before Pilate consists of seven paragraphs in the NRSV, which correspond to the seven episodes of the larger passage of the trial. The text as written strains credulity. Pilate, who was known for his cruelty, would have dispensed with Jesus quickly. He wouldn't have engaged in an extended dialogue with Jesus's accusers. And he certainly wouldn't have released a revolutionary to them, even if it was the "son of the father." The issue, however, is power, which is raised specifically in the next to last episode (19:8–12). Pilate says that he has power to release Jesus and power to crucify him. If that were true, Pilate would have already done it. Then why the dillydally? For one thing, Jesus needs to say his piece. He needs to say that the power to release or crucify Jesus has been given to Pilate from above, that is, from God. Then Jesus adds something confounding; he says, "The one who handed me over to you has the greater sin" (19:11). And who is that? God? Satan? Hmm.

The trial is part of the larger Passion Narrative, which comprises chapters 18 and 19. Jesus is arrested in a garden across the Kidron valley. (The place of Jesus's arrest in Matthew and Mark is called Gethsemane, Matt 26:36; Mark 14:32.) Then he is taken to the former high priest Annas (John 18:13, 19–23), then to the high priest Caiaphas (18:24), all the while Simon Peter is denying Jesus (18:15–18, 25–27). Jesus then goes to Pilate for an extended interrogation (18:28—19:16a), and then he is crucified in front of his mother, other women, and the beloved disciple (19:16b–37). Finally, Jesus is buried in a garden in a new tomb (19:38–42).

The Passion Narrative is part of a larger section in the Gospel, the "Book of Glory" (chs 13–20), in which Jesus speaks of his glorification through death, resurrection, and ascension and then John narrates it. In addition to the Passion Narrative, the "Book of Glory" contains the "Farewell Discourse" (chs. 13–17) and the Resurrection Narrative (ch. 20). Preceding the "Book of Glory" is the "Book of Signs" (1:19—12:50), in which Jesus displays miraculous signs that he is from God. Preceding the "Book of Signs" is the "Prologue" (1:1–18), in which the Word with God becomes the Word becomes flesh in Jesus. Following the "Book of Glory" is the "Epilogue" (ch. 20), in which the Risen Jesus appears to the disciples in Galilee.[2]

This Episode of the Trial

Pilate asks Jesus if he is King of the Jews (18:33). This is a strange question. If Jesus were King of the Jews, why would his "subjects" bring him to Pilate for execution? This title of "king" has been floating throughout the Gospel. At its beginning, Nathanael confesses that Jesus is the Son of God and the King of Israel (1:49). And Jesus does seem to be the broker of the kingdom of God (3:3, 5). But "king" is not Jesus's preferred title. After the feeding of the five thousand, the people want to take Jesus by force and make him king (6:15).

So now the title comes up again, on the lips of Pilate. If Jesus is a king, then he is a threat to Caesar, the true king. Pilate is so enamored with this title that he placards it on the cross in three languages, Hebrew, Latin and Greek (19:20). The priestly hierarchy protests, but Pilate shuffles away their objections as he has shuffled away Jesus.

Jesus does admit to having a reign, but it is "not from this world" (18:36). It is from above, from God (3:3, 7; 8:23). Pilate has caught Jesus, he thinks. If you've got a reign, then you are a king. Jesus says that those are Pilate's words. Jesus, however, frames his task differently: he has been born, he has come (from above) into this world to testify to the truth. Jesus defines his own role as a witness.

He is not the only one. John says that after Jesus died, a soldier's spear-pierced his side, and watery blood flowed. How do we know? The beloved disciple (BD) is Johnny on the spot in John: "The one who saw testified, so that you might believe, and his testimony is true, and that one knows that he speaks truth" (19:35). The BD also testifies to the truth, not just here at the cross, but also at the Sea of Tiberius when the Risen Jesus is speaking with Peter about shepherding and dying (21:15–23). John says, "This is the disciple who testifies concerning these things and has caused these things

2. I have taken this division from Brown, *Gospel According to John (I–XII)*.

to be written, and we know that his testimony is true" (21:24). The BD has a fan club, a community of BDs who give the stamp of approval to *the* BD. So we have a chain of witnesses, from Jesus, the True Truth-Testifier, to the BD, who lays in Jesus's bosom (13:23), just as the Son lays in the Father's bosom (1:18), to the community that endorses the truth of the BD's testimony.

Testifying is a key concept in John. In the beginning, when there is the Word (1:1), John the Baptist comes to testify to the light so that all might believe (1:6–7). The Gospel continues, "He himself was not the light, but he came to testify to the light" (1:8). So, at the beginning of the Gospel, John testifies to the light. Here near the end of the Gospel, Jesus says that his mission is to testify to the truth (18:37; see also 1:15). Indeed, in chapter 1 of this gospel, four times it says that the Baptist testified or gave testimony to Jesus (1:7–8, 19, 32). It's a testifying time in this Gospel. And Jesus is the main testifier in this Gospel. He is a witness, and not a witless witness. No, he's a very witty witness, because his testimony comes from God. He testifies to what he has seen and heard—from God—but alas, no one accepts his testimony. Poor little Jesus boy! His testimony is rejected! (3:32–33) He came into his own, and his own didn't accept him (1:11). But some did; some received his testimony (3:33) and became children of God (1:12). Oh boy! Oh girl! Oh, peeps! Why did "his own" not receive him? Why did others believe in his name?

People accept Jesus's witness, and they testify! That's what the Samaritan woman—the woman at the well—does (4:7–42). Jesus ain't got no bucket, but he's got living water, which the woman wants to drink up! Jesus tells her that she's had five husbands, and she runs and tells everybody, "Hey! Some dude told me everything I've ever done. He can't be the Messiah, can he?" (4:29). Yes, he can. And lots of Samaritans—lotsa Sammies—believe in Jesus because of the woman's testimony. "He told me ever'thing—I mean ever'thing—I ever done" (4:29). Apparently she hasn't done very much in her life because the only thing that Jesus has said about the woman is that she has had five husbands and was living with someone who was not her husband. A male relative? . . . the surviving fifth son of her first husband's mother? Nevertheless, she testifies. And the Sams say to Jesus that they don't need her testimony anymore because Jesus has stayed there two days and they believe that he's the Savior of the world (4:42). The world savior, the world savor. Jesus tastes mmm-mmm good!

Let's romp through the gospel on a testimony hunt. In chapter 5, the word group "testimony/testify" is prominent in verses 31–39. And the

Greek word here is μαρτυρία/μαρτυρέω. We get the word "martyr" from this word. And a martyr is a witness who is willing to die on account of his testimony. Martyrs also give testimony to a cause with their death.

"Testimony/testify" appears nine times in as many verses. In chapter 5, Jesus says that someone else testifies on his behalf: God. Yes, the man upstairs, or I mean, the person upstairs—God—whom Jesus constantly calls Father. So, Jesus has several witnesses: himself, John, Jesus's works, God, and the Scripture. So, Jesus is one of a bunch of witnesses.

These witnesses testify on Jesus's behalf, like a court scene. Indeed, it has been suggested that this Gospel was written when Jesus-believers were being hauled into court.[3] A popular discussion starter among church youth groups in the 1970s was the sentence, "If you were arrested for being a Christian, would there be enough evidence to convict you?" It was also the title of a popular gospel song. How would you witness, testify? Both are translations of the word group μαρτυρία/μαρτυρέω.

Jesus testifies against the world that its works are evil (7:7). You may say that all its works are not evil. But in this Gospel the world is going to hell in a handbasket. The world is in rebellion against God. Its works are evil. Jesus testifies against it, and therefore the world hates him. "Boo, Jesus, bad, for testifying against us," says the world. Jesus's brothers—and yes, Jesus had brothers—don't believe in him (7:5), and he says that the world doesn't hate them, but it hates him because of his testimony against the world.

Later, Jesus says that he's the light of the world (8:12), and the Pharisees complain. Ah, they're always complaining, aren't they? Buncha whiners! They say, "You're testifying on your own behalf, so your testimony is no good! Nah-nah-nah-nah!" (8:13). Jesus says that his testimony is good because he knows where he comes from and he knows where he is going. Jesus quotes the Jewish law (Deut 19:15) that says that a testimony is no good unless you have two witnesses (John 8:17). That makes sense. Jesus says that he's got two witnesses: himself, and the Father who sent him. And that's how Jesus names God: "the Father-who-sent-him." God is a sending God. And that sending God testifies on Jesus's behalf. The Pharisees don't know Jesus or his Father. And Jesus splits the scene from the temple treasury. Pity the poor Pharisees!

"The Jews" don't believe in Jesus, even though his works in his Father's name testify to him. They don't belong to his sheep (10:3). "Bah!"

---

3. See Harvey, *Jesus on Trial.*

Later in the Gospel, when Jesus huddles with his disciples and gives the "Farewell Discourse" (13:31—17:26), Jesus says that the Spirit of truth testifies on his behalf (15:26). It is the Advocate, Comforter, the one-called-alongside. And Jesus talks about testimony to truth while he is standing before Pilate (18:37). While he's standing before his disciples he talks about testimony to truth, about testifying to truth. The Spirit testifies to the truth. So the Spirit is another testifier, another witness. So we have a bunch of witnesses in this Gospel: the Baptist, Jesus, his works, the Father, the Scriptures (and we're talking about the Hebrew Scriptures, the Jewish Scriptures, the Christians' OT, which were read in Greek, what is now known as the Septuagint). And now we have a new witness: you. You might say, "me!?" Yes, you. You. You are a witness. Jesus is actually talking to his disciples at supper, but he means you. Since you're reading this Gospel. He later breathes on the disciples and sends them out in the Spirit of peace to be witnesses (20:22–23). To testify. On Jesus's behalf.

And now we come back to our focal passage, the trial before Pilate: Jesus's job is to testify to the truth (18:37). His word, which is God's word, is truth (17:17). The truth sets us free (8:32). His flesh is true bread and his blood true drink (6:55). He is the resurrection and the life (11:25), the way, the truth, and the life (14:6), the true vine (15:1). If we belong to the truth, we listen to Jesus's voice, and he becomes our good shepherd, calling us by name and leading us out of fear, of danger, of threats from the wolf (10:1–18).

Pilate, well, he's not one who belongs to the truth. He doesn't listen to Jesus's voice. Rather, he shakes his head and rolls his eyes. "What's truth?" he says (18:38). Hello! The truth is standing right there in front of you, Pilate. Don't you remember what Jesus said, that he is the truth? Oh, you probably haven't read that part of the Gospel, have you, Pilate? Well, it's true anyway. Even if you don't believe it.

We Have in the Gospel, Then,

a transmission of true testimony,
   from God the Creator
   to Jesus, who is truth,
   to the BD, who, as the Beloved, lies in Jesus's bosom at supper (13:23),
   to the DBD (BD's disciples) who writes these things down as the BD's
true testimony (21:24),

to me, who writes about what the DBD has written—Does that make me a DDBD, Disciple of the Disciple of the Beloved Disciple?—to you.

* What are you going to do with that testimony? I realize that that will depend on your context.

* Why are you reading this book? You may be reading it for a college, university, or seminary class. Or you may be reading it for a church book study. Or you may be reading it on your own.

* Nevertheless, the question remains: What are you going to do with this testimony?

* What might acceptance mean for you practically?

* What might rejection mean for you?

My testimony with the Gospel of John begins in the fall of 1978, when I walked into R. Alan Culpepper's classroom at eight o'clock in the morning for an elective in the Fourth Gospel at The Southern Baptist Theological Seminary in Louisville, Kentucky. That testimony continued with a dissertation entitled "Wisdom Christology in the Fourth Gospel," completed in 1985 and published in revised form in 1992. And it followed with a book entitled *Word and Soul: A Psychological, Literary, and Cultural Reading of the Fourth Gospel*, published in 2001. And now I have written a section of a chapter on the Gospel of John. In what way is my testimony true? In what way is it not?

At this writing (June 1, 2022), I have just finished up a five-sermon series on the Gospel of John, entitled "Being One." Following the Revised Common Lectionary, I preached on John 21:1–19, "Do You Love Me?"; John 10:22–30, "The Father and I Are One"; John 13:31–36, "Love One Another"; John 14:23–29, "Do Not Let Your Hearts Be Troubled"; and John 17:20–26, "That They May Be One." I am serving as interim pastor of Second Baptist Church, Suffield, Connecticut. The church called a settled pastor who will come in mid-September. My objective is to testify to the oneness to which the Gospel testifies, the oneness of Jesus and God, the oneness of the believer and Jesus, and the oneness of the believer with fellow believers in that congregation.

The church has had some challenges in the past, and some observers have said that challenges remain. I have said that the church can best prepare for a settled pastor by focusing on its oneness. It is easy for a church to focus on the disagreements or the divisions. There will always be disagreements, and these disagreements will at times be forcefully held. But what is the unity that underlies the diversity?

> Think of a group that you are part of. It can be a religious community, a civic organization, or a club. Where do you find unity in your group? Where do you find diversity? How does the group nurture that unity? How does it encourage diversity? Does your group have a mission statement? If so, how does it recognize unity in diversity?

Here is the mission statement of the church I currently serve:

> The grace of Jesus Christ calls us into a community of faith embracing God's justice and love for all. We draw upon the stories of the past for insight, the experiences of the present for instruction, and the hope of the future for inspiration. We welcome all who join us in this endeavor through worship, education, mission, and service in the name of Christ.[4]

* What do you think of this mission statement?

* Where is the unity?

* Where is the diversity?

* How is this mission statement like the statement for your group? How is it different?

* To what truth does your group testify?

* In what ways does it testify to that truth?

Select Recommended Resources:

Callahan, Allen Dwight. "John." In *True to Our Native Land: An African American New Testament Commentary*, edited by Brian K. Blount et al., 186–212. Minneapolis: Fortress, 2007.

Coloe, Mary L., et al. *John 1–10* and *John 11–21*. Wisdom Commentary Series 44. Collegeville, MN: Liturgical, 2021.

---

4. Second Baptist Church, "Mission Statement."

Harvey, A. E. *Jesus on Trial: A Study in the Fourth Gospel*. London: SPCK, 1976.

Newheart, Michael Willett. *Word and Soul: A Psychological, Literary, and Cultural Reading of the Fourth Gospel*. Collegeville, MN: Liturgical, 2001.

O'Day, Gail R. "John." In *Women's Bible Commentary*, edited by Carol Newsom et al., 517–30. Rev. ed. Louisville: Westminster John Knox, 2012.

Reinhartz, Adele. "The Gospel of John." In *The Jewish Annotated New Testament*, edited by Amy-Jill Levine and Mark Zvi Brettler, 168–218. New York: Oxford University Press, 2017.

Segovia, Fernando. "John." In *A Postcolonial Commentary on the New Testament Writings*, edited by Fernando F. Segovia and R. S. Sugirth-arajah, 156–93. Bible and Postcolonianism 13. London: T. & T. Clark, 2009.

Artistic Response to This Episode of the Trial before Pilate:

Watt Iz Trooth?

6

Liberating Pedagogy and Intersectional Trauma

Philip and the Ethiopian Eunuch (Acts 8:26–40)

By Mitzi J. Smith

AS AN INTERPRETATIVE GUIDE and model, this chapter provides an outline for reading the story of the Ethiopian Eunuch through the justice framework of liberative (as opposed to oppressive) pedagogy.[1] The chapter is organized similar to chapter 4. It includes a discussion of my context as interpreter and my reason for selecting the particular justice issue. Again, I name my reading approach as an Africana womanist perspective that privileges Black women's experiences and ways of knowing. I identify and summarize the focus passage, which is the story of the encounter between the evangelist Philip and the Ethiopian eunuch in Acts 8:26–40. I do not offer my own translation of Acts 8:26–40, but I encourage students with some ancient Greek language facility to translate the passage themselves or portions of it. Questions are raised of the text based on the justice framework, and I suggest resources for further building that interpretive lens. I analyze and interrogate or raise questions of the selected passage and discuss it within its literary context. Finally, I ask questions about the historical context and recommend secondary resources like Bible commentaries as

---

1. This outline is based on chapter 4, "Epistemologies, Pedagogies, and the Subordinated Other" of Smith, *Womanist Sass and Talk Back*.

dialogue partners. Again, our purpose is not to provide any extensive lists of resources but to provide examples.

Interpreter's Context and Selection of the Justice Issue

I began teaching in seminary in 2006, after completing my PhD. I was the only and first full-time tenure-track African American woman biblical scholar hired at my former institution, and I am the first African American woman biblical scholar tenured full professor at my current school. It is still rare that students in theological higher education are taught by African American women biblical scholars. In most seminaries and divinity schools, students can graduate without ever having sat in a biblical studies (and in other areas of religious studies) classroom where an African American woman was the instructor and never have read a textbook authored by an African American woman biblical scholar. White men are still regarded and treated as the authority in the classroom and in terms of biblical scholarship, which means women's and BIPOC people's authority, epistemologies or ways of knowing and knowledge production, and scholarship are suspect, ignored, diminished, and questioned. We are presumed incompetent. This lack of diversity and bias most likely means that students are not exposed to diverse voices and epistemologies or ways of knowing. Thus, the justice issue I select is oppressive pedagogical structures and practices that exclude, marginalize and silence diverse, overtly contextual, and nonwhite voices and their embodied presence. A liberative pedagogy is inclusive, dialogical, and radically diverse.

Africana Womanist Reading Approach

I continue to do biblical interpretation from an Africana womanist reading approach. I hermeneutically privilege the histories, artifacts, experiences, ways of knowing, pedagogies, knowledge production and wisdoms of Black women and our communities that engender and center liberation and freedom. In so doing I diverge from whitened biblical interpretation that imagines and normalizes its task as acontextual, apolitical, and non-theo-ideological. Womanist ethicist Katie Geneva Cannon asserted that womanist pedagogy disrupts "conventional and outmoded dominant theological resources, deconstructing ideologies that led us into complicity with our own oppression."[2]

Summary of Scripture and Discussion of Justice Framework

The Scripture passage/pericope that I have selected to interpret through the lens of and in conversation with liberative pedagogy is the story of the encounter between the evangelist Philip and the Ethiopian eunuch at Acts 8:26–40. In that story, the angel of the Lord and the Spirit orchestrate a meeting between the evangelist Philip and the eunuch on the Gaza road that leads away from Jerusalem (8:26, 29, 39). The Ethiopian had traveled to Jerusalem to worship and is returning in his chariot. While riding in his chariot, he is reading the scroll of Isaiah when Philip approaches him and asks him if he understands what he is reading. The Ethiopian's reply to Philip's question seems to imply that he doesn't understand and needs a hermeneutical guide. With the Ethiopian's permission Philip joins him in his chariot and explains to him that the person about whom he is reading is Jesus who was crucified. The Ethiopian is convinced that he needs to be baptized, asking what prevents Philip from baptizing him. Philip baptizes the Ethiopian and the latter continues his journey home, but the Spirit transports Philip away. The Ethiopian is not mentioned again in Acts.

Justice Framework

It matters who teaches and how we teach. Too often teaching, like evangelization, is about lecturing or disseminating and rehearsing information or knowledge. It's about pouring into minds as much information as they can hold and regurgitate on an exam. Critical engagement between student-teachers and teacher-students is not the norm. Too many students expect theological educators to affirm what they think they already know, and educators too often oblige with a banking-model of education whereby students are indoctrinated or simply receivers of information. Students often do not even know how to engage critically; they do not know how to raise questions. I have had students literally tell me that they don't even know what to ask. They do not know how to ask critical questions or lack the confidence

---

2. Cannon, *Katie's Canon*, 137.

in their ability or agency to raise questions. We enter the world as curious human beings with many questions, but our curiosity is stifled, discouraged and suppressed when we start school, if not before; we are taught to receive information, to learn answers, to listen, and to ask few questions. In his book *A More Beautiful Question*, Warren Berger argues that schools and other institutions do not encourage questions because "questions challenge authority and disrupt established structures, processes, and systems, forcing people to have to at least *think* about doing something differently. To encourage or even allow questioning is to cede power . . . a teacher must be willing to give up control to allow for more questioning."[3] A Facebook "friend" and comedian out of Chicago posted that he "went to church with his wife and I asked so many questions that they thought I was the devil." I found his post hilarious *and* sadly true.

Liberative education as a practice of freedom exists only where teachers encourage and make space for students' questions. And, as Paulo Freire argues, it is where students and teachers engage in critical dialogue and where teachers are learners and students are teachers.[4]

Further, students are often discouraged from knowing/constructing and privileging their own worldview, contexts, experiences when doing biblical interpretation. Freire argues that education that neglects critical consideration of the student's worldview or the worldview of the oppressed and does not reflect their locatedness in the world risks "preaching in the desert" or imposes a banking model that focuses on providing information to passive human vessels.[5]

Many biblical studies students understand biblical exegesis as the task of passively imbibing and/or stitching together information from commentaries written primarily, if not only, by white men. Of course, most commentaries or commentary series are written primarily by white men. And those commentaries, whether in a study Bible, a one-volume commentary or in a commentary series, are treated as *the* truth or final interpretive word. Even "students of color are accustomed to being taught by white male instructors who privilege white male scholarship as *the* normative [authoritative] and legitimate voice."[6] When we "educate" students to be passive receptacles of normalized whitened knowledge, we cannot expect them to become social

3. Berger, *More Beautiful Question*, 6.

4. Freire, *Pedagogy of the Oppressed*, 61–62.

5. Freire, *Pedagogy of the Oppressed*, 75, 77.

6. Smith, *Womanist Sass and Talk Back*, 55.

justice advocates or activists. We are helping to create a passive citizenry and leaders.

A liberative pedagogy is also a humanizing one. "Dialogue between students and teachers that values the prior knowledge that students bring to the learning process is the basis for a humanizing pedagogy. [A humanizing] pedagogy encourages critical engagement with others different from ourselves, not in order to dominate, but in pursuit of diverse dialogue partners."[7] It matters who, what, and why we require students to read. Barbara Omolade asserts that "the challenge of a Black feminist pedagogy is to use literature to connect people with ideas and histories across racial, gender, and class boundaries and to further connect Black women to each other and to their unique history."[8] The only critical engagement many students will have with a plurality of diverse voices across race, gender, ethnicity, and sexuality will be in a classroom where such voices are centered required reading. "Educators that value humanizing pedagogy will not be satisfied to simply supplement the majority malestream texts with minoritized voices but will attempt to create equity by decentering androcentric and majority whitestream perspectives and concerns."[9] And a textbook written by a Black man cannot speak for Black women. Nor can a text by a white woman take the place of texts that BIPOC women produce. And no one, two or three people from any demographic group can speak for all.

> When I (Newheart) was teaching at Saint Paul School of Theology in Kansas City, Missouri, in the late 1980s, I was required to include material written by BIPOC scholars as required texts. When I taught at HUSD, I continued this practice. I made sure that I included material written by women scholars and African American scholars as texts. As a white male professor, it is easy for me to give the impression that whitened "malestream" scholarship is all there is, so it is important that I center perspectives that are different from mine. In the same way, now that I am a pastor, it is important that in my preaching and teaching I include perspectives from women and persons of color.

7. Smith, *Womanist Sass and Talk Back*, 54.

8. Omolade, *Rising Song*, 133.

9. Smith, *Womanist Sass and Talk Back*, 54.

Questions That Emerge From the Justice Framework

1.   Have you had a negative or positive experience with asking questions in a classroom? If so, please share.

2.   What makes it easier or more difficult for you to ask questions in a classroom setting?

3.   What is your experience with asking questions in the biblical studies or religious studies classrooms?

4.   What is the relationship between the way we learn and how we engage in the world?

5.   Does centering the biblical text as historical artifact and the historical context of the biblical text hinder liberative pedagogy? If so, explain? If not, explain?

6.   How can the accreditation standards of the Association of Theological Schools and of other accrediting institutions facilitate and insure their constituents are delivering or engaged in liberative pedagogies?

7.   What structures and policies in courses you have taken or in theological schools resist liberative pedagogies?

8.   How do the small numbers of Black, Native Indigenous and other people of color (BIPOC) biblical scholars adversely impact or inhibit liberative pedagogies?

9.   How much does liberative pedagogy depend on the publications of BIPOC biblical scholars and what can theological schools do to assist BIPOC biblical scholars?

10. What might be some strengths and weaknesses of the banking model and the liberative model of pedagogy? What are the costs and benefits to the student? What are the costs and benefits to the teacher?

Select Helpful Resources For Constructing the Justice Framework

Perlow, Olivia N., et al., eds. *Black Women's Liberatory Pedagogies: Resistance, Transformation and Healing Within and Beyond the Academy.* New York: Palgrave McMillan, 2018.

Freire, Paulo. *Pedagogy of the Oppressed*. New York: Continuum, 1993.

hooks, bell. *Teaching to Transgress: Education as the Practice of Freedom.* New York: Routledge, 1994.

Niemann, Yolanda Flores, et al. *Presumed Incompetent II: Race, Class, Power, and Resistance of Women in Academia*. Logan, UT: Utah State University Press, 2020.

Picower, Bree. *Reading, Writing, and Racism: Disrupting Whiteness in Teacher Education and in the Classroom*. Boston: Beacon, 2021.

Segovia, Fernando F., and Mary Ann Tolbert, eds. *Teaching the Bible: The Discourses and Politics of Biblical Pedagogy*. Minneapolis: Fortress, 2009.

Analysis and Interrogation of the Focus Passage

We notice that one of the characters in our story is named and the other is anonymous. The one who is sent and who will teach is named; he is Philip. We know him first from Acts 6. The student in this story is identified by his nationality, gender, the trauma inflicted on his body, and his position in the queen's court: He is an Ethiopian; he is likely a male who has been castrated (probably against his will or by coercion); and he is a treasurer for the queen of Ethiopia or the Candace and has access to the queen's chariots or one of his own. We also know that he owns a scroll of Isaiah, that he can read the scroll, and that he is likely bilingual. The Ethiopian is probably reading the Greek translation of the Isaiah scroll and his native language is Ge'ez. The Ethiopian is a worshiper of the God of Israel who has traveled to the temple in Jerusalem and is returning home.

Concerning Philip we know that the Angel of the Lord and the Spirit guide and speak to him; he listens and follows their directions. Philip finds, as directed, the Ethiopian eunuch on the Gaza road leading away from Jerusalem. They meet on the margins of Jerusalem. Philip is familiar with the scroll of Isaiah. Philip knows how to baptize, and he baptizes the Ethiopian eunuch.

Questions of the Passage:

1. What was Philip doing before the angel of the Lord spoke to him? What do we know about Philip from Acts?

2. Why would Philip follow the angel of the Lord and not question what the angel tells him?

3. Who is the teacher and who is the student and how does this resemble the justice problem?

4. How would you describe this teaching event? As passive? As dialogical? As liberative? As a combination of passive and dialogical? Explain.

5. Why do you think the Ethiopian is so easily convinced that Jesus is the one about whom the prophet speaks?

6. What repetitions do you see in the text and what are the implications?

7. What is highlighted in the text? How is it highlighted? And what is the impact?

8. Where do you see a lack of diversity in the hermeneutical interaction/moment in the story?

9. What are we to make of the fact that the Ethiopian had the scroll of Isaiah?

10. Whose context and experience informs an interpretation of the Isaiah scroll? What is that context and experience?

11. What does the scroll testify about? Who else testifies in the passage and how?

12. Who is silenced and how?

13. If you read Greek, what patterns do you see in the language of the Greek that you do not see in English translations like the NRSV, NRS-Vue, CEB?

14. If you read Greek, what might you translate differently from existing English translations and what difference does it make?

15. Many more questions can be asked of this text and of the text as it relates to the justice issue. Raise at least six more questions.

A note about Greek: We have witnessed too many students who have not learned Greek use a concordance to identify the Greek word being translated in English and provide the translation offered in the concordance. We do not find that helpful, and normally it adds no value to an interpretation paper. Persons who have studied Greek should use a current theological dictionary that gives a range of meanings in their various contexts. But keep in mind, there is no final interpretive word. We can also do our own comparative contextual work. For example, look up the word *rejoice* in an English translation of the Acts of the Apostles, including the occurrence in the passage we are examining in this chapter. Next, check each occurrence in the Greek text to see if the same or different Greek words are being translated. Finally, examine the context (in English, or Greek if you can) of each occurrence. How does the context impact the meaning? Would you translate each instance the same? Another exercise would be to look up the word *love* in an English translation in the Gospel of John and then look at each instance in the Greek text to see if they are the same Greek word. Finally, read each instance in its literary context. Sometimes we note that students simply state the Greek word, e.g., "The word Paul (or John) uses here for love is *agape*." That statement alone adds nothing to the paper. Does Paul (or John) use other words for love? If so, where and in what context? The student seems to think that simply identifying the Greek word is instructive, but it's not. Students should use Greek only when they themselves know it and know how to use it responsibly!

The Literary Context and Comparative Stories

The *immediate literary context* of Acts 8:26–40 is the cohesive episode that precedes it, which is Acts 8:1–25 and that which follows it, namely Acts 9:1–19. What connections (e.g., themes, repetitions, words, phrases, characters) do you see across the three episodes that contribute to an understanding of Acts 8:26–40? What interpretative or knowledge gaps do Acts 8:1–25 (Philip and Simon story) and Acts 9:1–19 (call of Saul/Paul) fill for Acts 8:26–40? Acts 8:1–25 tells us why and how we find Philip in Samaria and/or outside of Jerusalem. The persecution, of which Saul plays a part, ignited after Stephen's speech forced Philip and others (except the Twelve) out of Jerusalem to begin the next geographical stage of the spread of the testimony about Jesus Christ (1:8). Saul/Paul is introduced in chapter 8 and his Damascus road call narrative is inserted after the Ethiopian eunuch's story, so that Saul/Paul frames the testimony about Philip's testimony among the people in Samaria and to the Ethiopian. Paul's call narrative directly follows the Ethiopian's story. Perhaps, Acts wants the reader to see the story of the Ethiopian and Saul/Paul as parallel accounts, so that both are call narratives (of a Jewish man and a gentile man?). After the baptism, the Spirit transports Philip away, but the Ethiopian eunuch goes on his way rejoicing (Greek: ἐπορεύετο γὰρ τὴν ὁδὸν αὐτοῦ χαίρων) (8:39). Three verses later, Paul/Saul is arresting men and women of the Way (ὁδοῦ) (9:2). Their paths are connected, but they do not meet.

Also in the preceding literary context, Philip's miracles and testimony are well received and result in the baptism of women and men, but the Spirit does not appear on its own (8:11–17). Instead, Peter and John, unaffected by the persecution that made Philip flee Jerusalem, travel to Samaria after hearing that Philip's converts had not received the Spirit. The two apostles, pray and lay hands on the new converts and they receive the Spirit, as if the Spirit arrives when it is summoned through the prayers of the Jerusalem apostles. However, in the story of the Ethiopian eunuch and Philip, the Spirit calls the shots and is in control.

What are we to make of this comparison? It is clear from the beginning of Acts and throughout that Jerusalem is to be regarded as the headquarters of the post-exaltation ministry even as the testimony about Jesus spreads beyond Jerusalem and Judea, and this hierarchy is demonstrated in various episodes, including the relationship between the Seven including Philip and the Twelve, as well as the pivotal story of Paul/Saul at the Jerusalem Council in chapter 15. We could make many more connections between the immediate literary context and our story, but we will stop here, and leave the rest to you, dear reader.

I identify the literary form, for purposes of comparison, of Acts 8:26–40 as a baptismal narrative or a conversion story. It is similar to other baptismal narratives and/or conversion stories in the Acts of the Apostles. Arguably, the story of the conversion of the Ethiopian is the first about a gentile convert in Acts, depending on whether or not one considers him to be a gentile or that a castrated man can convert. We have no idea at what point in his life he was castrated; it is not impossible that he is Jewish. In the conversion story of the gentile centurion Cornelius, Peter baptizes him and his household (Acts 10). When Cornelius is converted, his entire household receives the Spirit and is then baptized, in that order (10:44–48; cf. Lydia and her household and the jailer and his family, Acts 16). The Ethiopian's baptism does not take place in his native country or in his home; he will return home, to a country that represented one of the ends or extremes of the Earth.[10] The Spirit is present and active before and after the Ethiopian's baptism, but it is not depicted as falling on him and does not explicitly say he received it (8:29, 39). Thus, the conversion and baptism of the Ethiopian fits the pattern of the Spirit's involvement in the Acts narrative, which, I argue, is unpredictable!

Understanding Our Text Within the Broader Literary Context of Acts

Beyond the immediate literary context mentioned above, the larger literary context of Acts can help us interpret the story of the encounter between Philip and the Ethiopian. What is it that we do not know and perhaps learn from the larger literary context of Acts? We can explore the following questions. *After each question, we must ask the "so what" question: what are the hermeneutical or interpretative implications for our passage?*

1. Who is Philip in Acts? (We asked this above, but we ask it here again.)

2. How does what is said about Philip elsewhere in Acts disagree or agree with the way he is characterized in our passage?

3. What is the significance of Jerusalem in Acts? What gentiles and what nationalities worship at the Jerusalem temple in Acts?

4. Where else is the word "eunuch" found in Acts, if at all? Where else are Ethiopia/Ethiopian and related words mentioned in Acts and what are the implications for our text?

10. Byron, *Symbolic Blackness and Ethnic Difference*, 31.

5. What are other instances of one-on-one teaching in Acts? Compare them.

6. What other instances of the word "hinder" do we find in Acts? Is it similar to or different from its use in our story?

7. How does the angel of the Lord behave differently or the same in our passage as in other stories in Acts?

8. How does the Spirit behave differently or the same in our passage as in other stories in Acts?

9. Where does the story of Philip and the Ethiopian fit in the geographical structure of Acts at 1:8?

10. Where or how does our story fit in the theology of Acts at 5:33–39?

11. What or who is a Godfearer in Acts and what can that tell us about the Ethiopian?

Students should attempt to address one or two of the most significant questions they raise about the relationship between their passage and its broader literary context. For the purposes of this chapter, I will address questions numbered 1, and 8 above.

Who is Philip in Acts? Philip emerges in Acts 6:1–6 where the Hellenist widows are being neglected in the table service (διακονεῖν τραπέζαις). The apostles' solution is the selection of seven testifying brothers, men (ἄνδρας) who are full of wisdom and of the Spirit to dedicate to the table ministry, while the twelve focus on preaching the word of God (6:2–3). Philip, along with Stephen, is one of the seven. Thus, he is known in the community as an absolutely wise and spirit-led/filled man, as demonstrated in his encounter with the Ethiopian. What that means is another question for Acts. The apostles, with the support of the entire community of disciples, anoint the seven, including Philip for that ministry. Yet, the spirit has other plans because both Stephen and Philip are powerful preachers of the gospel in Acts; they testify. Stephen gives the longest speech in Acts and is stoned to death for it (ch. 7). After which the seven or the Hellenists (Greek speaking Jews) are persecuted and forced to flee Jerusalem (8:1–3). That Philip witnessed Stephen's murder, endured persecution, was forced to flee represents a lot of physical, spiritual, and emotional trauma. Yet, because of the dispersion, Philip finds himself in Samaria where he is instrumental in the conversion of Simon Magus (8:4–25) and then is sent to meet the Ethiopian. Despite that the community limited the seven to table ministry,

Philip (and Stephen) preach the gospel successfully to people who, like them, live on the margins of society—a well-meaning Simon and the eager and vulnerable Ethiopian eunuch. Philip could identify with both of his converts. Philip is a wounded and traumatized witness. And it is in the context of his traumatized self and community that Philip testifies to the Ethiopian about Jesus Christ. Although a disciple of Isaiah or Trito-Isaiah (53:7–8) referred to a historical person, community, and/or ideal suffering servant, Jesus becomes the silent suffering lamb who was denied justice and finally killed in Philip's testimony to the eunuch's question: I beg of you, about whom does the prophet say this? About himself or about someone else? (8:34). The Ethiopian asks what he does not know. His question reveals he is conscious of what he does not know. In response and taking the Isaiah passage as his point of department, Philip testifies about Jesus. We don't learn unless we can ask questions, but one answer should not end the inquiry. It is the Ethiopian who asks a second question as the chariot approaches a body of water: "Look, water! What precludes me from being baptized?" (8:36). Philip's initial question, "Do you comprehend what you are reading?" (8:30) sparked the Ethiopian's other question: "How can I unless someone should guide me?" (8:31). From that point, Philip assumed the role of testifying-teacher. The Ethiopian is depicted as the receiver of the testimony and the student with questions to which he is given single-answers that he unequivocally accepts as true.

The second question I will address is *How is the behavior of the Spirit in the story of Philip and the Ethiopian different from or similar to elsewhere in Acts?* While you will find later that some commentators argue that the Ethiopian eunuch was not the first gentile convert (some argue that he was not a gentile, others that the Spirit did not anoint him and so on), we find that there is no one way that the Spirit performs or shows up, if it does, in baptism or conversion narratives in Acts. In the narrative of Cornelius immediately following the Ethiopian's story, the Spirit anoints Cornelius and his household *before* their baptism (10:44–48), which is different from what happened at Pentecost (2:37–40). In the Ethiopian's narrative, the Spirit is present from beginning to end; it does not leave the scene until after the baptism. The Spirit is unpredictable in Acts, and for that reason the story of the Ethiopian fits the pattern of the Spirit elsewhere in Acts.

Questions about Historical Context and Some Recommended Resources

What is it that we do not know about the historical context of this story? Do not presume to know because someone preached a sermon or taught a Bible study on the topic? Do not assume that no one has produced any new or different information, knowledge or opinions worth pursuing than those you think you already know. Here are some questions to consider:

1. What is a eunuch?

2. What can we know about eunuchs from the Old Testament and other ancient literature? (See, e.g., Deut 23:1–8; Isa 56:3–5.)

3. How was a person made a eunuch? What was the impact of on his life? Whom did it benefit?

4. What is the relationship between Ethiopia and the Roman Empire during the first and early second centuries CE? And what bearing might that have on an interpretation of this story?

5. What is a scroll? In what language was the scroll that the eunuch was reading and what are the implications?

6. What can we know about the ancient first-century Gaza road? What are the implications for our story?

7. What can we know about first-century Jewish baptisms?

8. How did an eunuch engage in worship at the Jerusalem temple? How was he limited?

9. How did society view eunuchs? Could one tell a person was a eunuch based on his outward appearance, clothing, or position?

10. Were eunuchs serving in the royal courts educated or literate?

11. What can we know about the history of Christianity in Ethiopia and what bearing might it have on this story?

Select Resources for Addressing Historical Context Questions

In addition to the Old Testament/Hebrew Bible and InterVarsity Press's *Dictionary of the Old Testament* series, I recommend the following texts:

Byron, Gay L. *Symbolic Blackness and Ethnic Difference in Early Christian Literature: Early Christian Ethno-Political Rhetorics about Egyptians, Ethiopians, Blacks and Blackness.* London: Routledge, 2002.

Esler, Philip. *Ethiopian Christianity: History, Theology and Practice.* Waco, TX: Baylor University Press, 2019.

Tougher, Shaun. *The Castrasti: Eunuchs in the Roman Empire.* New York: Bloomsbury, 2022.

Dialogue with Secondary Resources

As a reminder, Bible commentaries, book chapters, and journal articles should only be consulted as dialogue partners and after the student has analyzed the passage under consideration and read it with attention to the immediate literary context and in its broader literary context.

Select Commentaries, Monographs, and Other Resources:

Burke, Sean D. *Queering the Ethiopian Eunuch.* Minneapolis: Fortress, 2013.

Kurtz, William S., SJ, et al. *Acts of the Apostles.* Catholic Commentary on Sacred Scripture Series. Grand Rapids: Baker, 2014.

Liew, Tat-Siong Benny. *What Is Asian American Biblical Hermeneutics? Reading the New Testament.* Honolulu: University of Hawai'i Press, 2008.

Maloney, Linda M., et al. *Acts of the Apostles.* Wisdom Commentary Series 45. Minneapolis: Liturgical, 2022.

Martin, Clarice J. "Acts of the Apostles." In *Searching the Scriptures: A Feminist Commentary,* edited by Elisabeth Schüssler Fiorenza, 2:763–99. New York: Crossroad, 1994.

Martin, Dale B. *Pedagogy of the Bible: An Analysis and Proposal.* Louisville, KY: Westminster John Knox, 2008.

Matthews, Shelly. *First Converts: Rich Pagan Women and the Rhetoric of Mission in Early Judaism and Christianity.* Stanford: Stanford University Press, 2001.

Newsom, Carol A., et al. *Women's Bible Commentary*. Rev. ed. Louisville, KY: Westminster John Knox, 2012.

Pervo, Richard I. *Acts of the Apostles*. Hermeneia. Minneapolis: Fortress, 2009.

Smith, Abraham. "A Second Step in African Biblical Interpretation: Generic Reading Analysis of Acts 8:26–40." In *Reading from This Place: Social Location and Biblical Interpretation in the United States*, edited by Fernando F. Segovia and Mary Ann Tolbert, 1:213–28. Minneapolis: Fortress, 1995

Thomaskutty, Johnson, et al., eds. *An Asian Introduction to the New Testament*. Minneapolis: Fortress, 2022.

Williams, Demetrius K. "Acts of the Apostles." In *True to Our Native Land: An African American Commentary of the New Testament*, edited by Brian K. Blount et al., 213–48. Minneapolis: Fortress, 2007.

The Baptism of the Ethiopian Eunuch

7

Testifying Paul Sings the Kenotic (Kinetic) Hymn

(Philippians 2:1–11)

By Michael Newheart

We now turn our attention to the epistles, specifically the Pauline epistles, the seven epistles that are regarded as "authentic" (Rom, 1–2 Cor, Gal, Phil, Phlm, 1 Thess). I am investigating perhaps the most widely investigated Pauline passage, Phil 2:6–11, a pericope that has often been called the "kenotic hymn" because the Greek word translated "emptied" in verse 7 is ἐκένωσεν (κενόω in its dictionary form). And it is called a "hymn" because it is often argued that this passage was originally a pre-Pauline hymn that Paul has adapted to his letter.[1] I find this issue fascinating because I like to imagine the early Jesus-believers singing this "hymn" in worship as testimony to their experience of Christ. Alas, the weight of scholarly opinion seems to have swung so that it is now considered a piece of Pauline poetic prose.[2] Nevertheless, the passage is "hymnic," and I will still refer to it as a "hymn."

---

1. Three important studies are: Lohmeyer, *Kyrios Jesus*; Käsemann, "Critical Analysis of Philippians 2:5–11"; Martin, *Hymn of Christ*.

2. See Gordley, *New Testament Christological Hymns*.

The emphasis in this chapter, however, is not to debate whether Phil 2:6–11 was originally a pre-Pauline hymn but to examine the passage as an example of Pauline testimony. To what is he testifying? Why is he testifying?

Verses 6–11 cannot be understood apart from its context. (Context is everything, remember?) I will investigate the passage, then, in the context of verses 1–5 in chapter 2 of the letter to the Philippians, and then in the context of the entire letter. I have printed my translation (Newheart Standard Version, "NSV") of verses 1–11 below.

Please stand and read it aloud. (Yes, right now, wherever you are.) Feel free to gesture and move around as you like. Indeed, be conscious of your voice and your body.

The Hymn

If then there is any encouragement in the Messiah,
If there is any comfort of love,
If there is any collaboration of spirit,
If there is any affection or compassion,

Fill up my joy in thinking the same,
Having the same love,
United in spirit,
Being one-minded,

Doing nothing according to selfish ambition or empty conceit,
But in humility treating one another better than yourselves.
Not looking out for yourselves
But for the interests of one another.

Have this mind among you that was also in Messiah Jesus,
who,
though existing in the form of God,
did not consider being equal with God
a thing to be grasped,
but emptied himself,
taking the form of a slave.
Becoming in human likeness,

And being found in human appearance,
he humbled himself,
becoming obedient to death,
death on a cross even.

Therefore,
God has super-exalted him
and graciously granted to him
the name that is above every name,
that at the name of Jesus
every knee shall bow,
in heaven and on the earth and under the earth,
and every tongue shall confess that
the Master is Jesus Messiah
to the glory of God the Creator.

Please respond to the following questions:

* So how was that?
* What words did you speak more loudly?
* What words did you speak more softly?
* What movements did you make?
* To what words did you make them?

(You might want to write the answers to these questions in a journal.)

I remember back in the late 1980s when I was teaching a course in New Testament Christology at Saint Paul School of Theology in Kansas City, Missouri, I had students stand and move their bodies to this passage as I read it aloud. A student approached me after class and said that she didn't like the ending "God the Father," which, she said, "was like a blow in the stomach." Ouch! In the translation above, I have changed the translation to "God the Creator." How does that translation make a difference?

The Hymn in Its Literary Context

Now, read silently the whole book of Philippians. It's only a few pages long. Write down your thoughts in response to these questions:

* What did you notice?

* How does 2:1–11 fit into the flow of the entire book of Philippians?

I notice that Paul is imprisoned (1:7, 13, 14, 17). He particularly wants his readers to know this fact right from the beginning of the letter. His imprisonment forms the context from which he writes. I also observe that Paul feels particularly close to this congregation, as demonstrated in the prayer in 1:3–11, in which he says that they hold him in their heart (1:7) and that he longs for them "with the compassion of Messiah Jesus" (1:8). Furthermore, near the end of the letter, he refers to the congregation as his "joy and crown" and that he loves them and longs for them (4:1).

Consider Paul's notion that he is imprisoned. In four NT letters, Paul claims to be in prison: Philippians, Philemon (1, 9), Colossians (4:3), and Ephesians (3:1; 4:1). Scholars have long questioned whether Colossians and Ephesians were in fact written by Paul because their vocabulary, theology, and historical situation seem to differ so much from other epistles, such as Romans and 1–2 Corinthians.[3] Also, in Colossians and Ephesians, "Paul as prisoner" appears to be a trope, a literary fiction that these two books are employing.

In Philippians, Paul is certainly in prison, and it forms an important part of the context of the letter. We will come back to this subject of Paul as imprisoned person, but we will first ask a few more questions concerning the hymn.

* How does Paul's context in prison help shape the context of the hymn?

* How does this hymn function in relation to the ancient system of enslaving and enslaved?

* What might this hymn say to those of African, Asian, or European descent, that is, those whose ancestors were enslaved?

* In Phil 2:10, near the end of the hymn, Paul quotes Isa 45:23. Read it aloud from Isaiah. What is the context of this passage in Isaiah?

* What does Paul do to the Isaiah passage by quoting it in his hymn?

* Paul also quotes Isa 45:23 in Rom 14:11. How does the Isaiah passage function there? How does its appearance in Romans compare to the hymn in Philippians?

---

3. Concannon, "Paul and Authorship."

* What does the hymn mean in the context of religious pluralism, such as we have today?

* In what sense are adherents of Allah, Yahweh, Buddha, Krishna forced to worship Master Jesus?

* What does the hymn say about religious freedom?

* In what sense are people humbling themselves to the capitalist economy?

* In what sense is this "sweet bye-and-bye" theology?

* In what sense does this hymn teach "poor now but rich in heaven"? How does the hymn help believers deal with contemporary earthly life?

* The climactic phrase reads in the Greek, "κύριος Ἰησοῦς Χριστὸς," "Jesus Christ is Lord."

* Or as Jerome Neyrey has it, "The Lord is Jesus Christ."[4] Try on different ways of saying this confession: Jesus Christ is Lord, The Lord is Jesus Christ. Lord Jesus Christ. Master Jesus Messiah. The Master is Jesus Messiah. Master Yesou Anointed. How are these translations different? How are they the same?

* What difference does it make to say, "Have this mind among you" as opposed to say, "Have this mind in you"?

Paul says in verse 7 that "Jesus emptied himself." Sallie McFague wrote about the self-emptying of Christ in a 2010 article about money and capitalism.

> This is an inversion of the usual understanding of power as control. Instead, power is given to others to live as diverse and valuable creatures. In the incarnation, as Paul writes in Philippians 2:7, God "emptied himself, taking the form of a slave," substituting humility and vulnerability for our insatiable appetites. In the cross God gives of the divine self without limit to side with the poor and the oppressed. God does not take the way of the victor but, like Jesus and the temptations, rejects absolute power and imperialism for a different way. Therefore, Christian discipleship becomes a "cruciform" life, imitating the self-giving of Christ for others.[5]

4. Neyrey, *Christ Is Community*, 219.
5. McFague, "Earth Economy."

Similarly, Michael Gorman sees Phil 2:6–11 as Paul's "master story." Gorman identifies "resurrectional cruciformity" as the center of Paul's thought.[6]

> For Paul, to be in Christ is to be a living exegesis of this narrative of Christ, a new performance of the original drama of exaltation following humiliation, of humiliation as the voluntary renunciation of rights and selfish gain in order to serve and obey. *Paul's spirituality of cruciformity is a narrative* spirituality, and the master narrative that shapes his spirituality is Philippians 2:6–11.[7]

For Further Scholarly Work on This Hymn, See These Commentaries:

Agosto, Efrain. "Philippians." In *A Postcolonial Commentary on the New Testament Writings*, edited by Fernando F. Segovia and R. S. Sugirtharajah, 281–93. London: T. & T. Clark, 2009.

Cook, Michael. "The Letter of Paul to the Philippians." In *The Jewish Annotated New Testament*, edited by Amy-Jill Levine and Mark Zvi Brettler, 354–62. 2nd ed. New York: Oxford University Press, 2017.

Fee, Gordon D. *Paul's Letter to the Philippians*. The New International Commentary on the New Testament. Grand Rapids: Eerdmans, 1995.

Stubbs, Monya. "Philippians." In *True to Our Native Land: An African American New Testament Commentary*, edited by Brian K. Blount, 363–79. Minneapolis: Fortress, 2007.

Tamez, Elsa, et al. *Philippians, Colossians, Philemon*. Wisdom Commentary Series 51. Collegeville, MN: Liturgical, 2017.

Works, Carla Swafford. "Philippians." In *Women's Bible Commentary*, edited by Carol Newsom et al., 581–84. Louisville, KY: Westminster John Knox, 2012.

According to the hymn, Jesus emptied himself by taking the form of an enslaved person. I think that this is metaphorical.[8] Jesus was enslaved

---

6. Gorman, "Paul and the Cruciform Way."

7. Gorman, *Cruciformity*, 92.

8. Mitzi Smith, however, argues that this reference is both literal and metaphorical, that Jesus was in fact depicted as an enslaved person in Luke's Gospel, at least, and the hymn is a second witness that Jesus entered the world, i.e., was born, an enslaved child.

to the powers as human beings were. While he was in the form of God and equal to God, Jesus held mastery over the powers; the powers were enslaved to him. But when he emptied himself of being in the form of God, he became enslaved to the powers, especially the power of death.

But Jesus did not die of "natural causes." Rather, his was "death on a cross" (v. 8). It is here that the Roman empire rears its ugly head, for crucifixion was the Roman penalty for treason or sedition. "The cross" for Paul is shorthand for Jesus's death "for us" or "for our sins," which is the message that Paul has received from others and passes on to his readers and hearers (1 Cor 15:3).

* To what extent is humanity in general enslaved to the powers?

* To what powers do you especially feel enslaved?

In many ways, Paul followed the kenotic lifestyle. Although he certainly was not equal to God, he did enjoy certain credentials, which he recites in 3:5–6: circumcised Israelite, Benjamite, Pharisee, persecutor of the church. Yet he emptied himself. He was a Roman prisoner (1:13); his life was poured out as a libation (2:17); he suffered the loss of all things (3:8).

The hymn turns on the conjunction "therefore" (v. 8, Greek διό). Jesus emptied himself, humbled himself, and as a result—therefore—God super-exalted him. This super-exaltation takes place in that God gives Jesus a name that is above every name.

And that name seems to be "Master" (or "Lord" as it is often translated, v. 11). "The Master is Jesus (Messiah)" (or "Jesus is Lord") seems to have been the characteristic confession of the early Jesus-believers (see Rom 10:9; 1 Cor 12:3b). Disciples were pledging their allegiance not to a human master but to the divine Master, Jesus Messiah. Indeed, Paul often begins and ends his letters with reference to Master Jesus Messiah, as he does here in Philippians (1:2; 4:23).

The Philippian hymn, then, is Paul's testimony to his Master Jesus Messiah. In the context of Roman imprisonment, Paul is testifying about his own humiliation and exaltation with Jesus. By including this hymn in his letter, Paul bends the knee with all creation and confesses Master Jesus Messiah (2:10–11). And Paul presents Jesus's example and Paul's own example to the Philippians. They too are to humble themselves as Jesus humbled himself (2:3, 8). They are to have the same mind with one another

---

She argues that it is not impossible that the historical Jesus himself was enslaved and later freed. See Smith, "Abolitionist Messiah," 53–70.

as they have the same mind as Jesus (2:2, 5). Indeed, this note of being "same-minded" appears several times in the letter (1:27; 3:15). It is not a surprise because early on, Paul lets us know of division at Philippi; there is "envy and rivalry" (1:5). He even identifies Euodia and Syntyche, women leaders in the Philippian church, and urges them "to be same-minded in the Master" (4:2–3). Unity, then, is an important theme in Paul's letter to the Philippians.

I remember that my seminary professor James L. Blevins used to say that the theme of Philippians was "not joy with a smiling face but joy in suffering." Yes, Paul was suffering; he was in a Roman prison, and out of this context he writes.

The Hymn in its Contemporary Context

Prison letters have long been considered as authoritative texts. Here are a few modern collections of prison letters:

Adayfi, Mansoor. *Don't Forget Us Here: Lost and Found at Guantanamo.* New York: Hachette, 2021.

Bonhoeffer, Dietrich, *Letters and Papers from Prison.* Edited by Victoria Barnett. Minneapolis: Fortress, 2015.

Jackson, George. *Soledad Brother: The Prison Letters of George Jackson.* Chicago: Lawrence Hill, 1994.

Jingsheng, Wei. *The Courage to Stand Alone: Letters from Prison and Other Writings.* New York: Viking, 1997.

Mandela, Nelson. *Prison Letters.* New York: Liveright, 2019.

Wituska, Krystyna. *Inside a Gestapo Prison: The Letters of Krystyna Wituska, 1942–1944.* Edited by Irene Tomaszewski. Detroit: Wayne State University Press, 2006.

Choose a few of these titles. Find out as much as you can about them on the internet.

  * In what ways do they echo the sentiments in Paul's letters?

  * In what ways are they distinct?

* Who do you know that is a prisoner, that is, they are under the supervision of the criminal justice system?

* What is their situation? If you feel so led, write them.

* Look at the website of Healing Communities, USA which addresses prison reentry, sexual exploitation, and juvenile justice awareness.[9] What hints of humiliation on the one hand and exaltation on the other do you see on the website?

As noted in chapter 5, I have had two realms of experience with the criminal justice system. First, I participated in AVP worships. Second, I exchanged correspondence for several years with Freddy Chacon, who was in solitary confinement (known as "the SHU," Secure Housing Unit) at Pelican Bay State Prison in California. Pelican Bay was listed in 2013 as one of the ten worst prisons in the country, according to *Mother Jones* magazine. The SHU is described this way:

> At Pelican Bay, the state's first and most notorious supermax, the 1,500 occupants of the Security Housing Unit (SHU) and Administrative Housing Unit spend 22.5 hours a day alone in windowless cells measuring about 7 x 11 feet. The remaining 90 minutes are spent, also alone, in bare concrete exercise pens. With no phone calls allowed, and only the rare noncontact visit, these prisoners . . . can only access the world outside their cells via their "feeding slots." And their only interactions with fellow prisoners consists of shouting through steel mesh—until the guards order them to shut up.[10]

I began writing Freddy in 2008. I corresponded with him through a program called Prison Pen Pals, through Sandy Spring (Maryland) Friends Monthly Meeting of the Baltimore Yearly Meeting of the Religious Society of Friends (Quakers). When I started writing him, Freddy had been in the SHU ten years, and he had the sentence of juvenile life without parole. Freddy received this sentence because he had taken a hostage while trying to escape from a juvenile detention center, and he was in the SHU because he was accused of having connections to gang members.[11] I thought,

9. Healing Communities USA.

10. Ridgeway and Casella, "America's 10 Worst Prisons: Pelican Bay."

11. See Fountain, "Man Sentenced to Life." Freddy and his accomplice were in a youth detention facility in California. Freddy fashioned a weapon and threatened to harm the facility's librarian if he and his accomplice were not given a truck to escape. While he was driving out of the facility, a guard sprayed mace into the cab of the truck through

"Wow! Life doesn't get much worse than this." To use the language of the hymn, Freddy had emptied himself. Indeed, he had not done so voluntarily, as Jesus is depicted as doing. Rather, "his [Freddy's] life was taken away" (Acts 8:33). Alas, I thought, Freddy would spend his life in prison as punishment for his crimes.

When Freddy began writing me, I was struck with his positive attitude. During our correspondence, Freddy became a Christian. He was very nonspecific, however, about the process. Nevertheless, I loved his letters. He had really turned himself around. His "super-exaltation" began while he was still imprisoned. He had accepted his fate; he was sorry for what he had done; he was determined to make the best that he could of his life.

In 2012 the US Supreme Court declared that juvenile life without parole was unconstitutional.[12] That same year, California Governor Jerry Brown allowed those who were sentenced to juvenile life without parole to have a hearing if they had served twenty years of their sentence. Freddy's accomplice was freed in 2014, and Freddy came up for a hearing in 2015. He testified how he felt regretful about his action. The woman that he had taken hostage said that she was going to testify that he should stay in prison, but when she heard his testimony, she was convinced that he should be free.

Freddy was then freed. He returned to his native Tijuana, Baja California, Mexico and started his own businesses, Fast Global Coverage and Fast Hunt Services. He has married and has a son.[13]

Freddy has a great testimony. He emptied himself, from the youth detention facility to taking the hostage to crashing the truck to Pelican Bay to the SHU. But God has "super-exalted" him, from Freddy's determination to better himself even though in the SHU to his hearing to his being freed to his returning to Tijuana to his starting these businesses to having a son. Yes, God has "super-exalted" him. On his Facebook page, Freddy writes in his introduction, "and so the unexpected happened!" And so it did! So it did.

---

a half-open window, and the truck crashed into a tree. Freddy and his accomplice were easily brought back into custody.

12. Rovner, "Juvenile Life without Parole: An Overview." "In 2012, deciding *Miller* [v. *Alabama*] and *Jackson* [v. Hobbs] jointly, the US Supreme Court held that, for people under eighteen years old, mandatory life without parole sentences violate the Eighth Amendment."

13. See Freddy's Facebook page, "Freddy Chacon del Real." I have his permission to share his story.

A Poetic Response to the Hymn

Here is a poem I recently wrote based on Paul's kenotic hymn:

Same mind, same mind, same love,
Same humble love,
Messiah Jesus God-form and God-equal,
Slave-form took he, looky, looky, looky.
Self-emptied, M.Teed, and did he bleed,
Cross-obedient, cross-death,
Cross-humble in his cross-trek.

And God-'xalted and above-named,
Name-upon-name-upon-name
'til they get to Jesus.
You hear me? JESUS! G-ZUS!
Now bent knee (and glee)
Heaven-earth-subterranean knee.
Tongues afire: MESSIAH JESUS!
MASTER JESUS!
Creator glory, God-dy glory,
Gory glory!
Glory! Glory!
Glory! Hallelujah!
And his soul goes marching on!
(Hit it, Pete!)

8

The Precarious Nature of Citizenship for the Marginalized

(Ephesians 2:11–22)

By Mitzi J. Smith

What one does not remember is the serpent in the garden of one's dreams . . . And memory makes its only real appearance in this life as this life is ending—appearing, at last, as a kind of guide into a condition which is as far beyond memory as it is beyond imagination . . . having once been a Black child in a White country. My memory stammers: but my soul is a witness.

— James Baldwin[1]

---

1. Baldwin, *Evidence of Things Not Seen*, xv. In this book Baldwin masterfully analyzes the crises of the missing twenty-eight children of Atlanta and race/racism in the context of a Southern city in the US. "*The spirit of the South is the spirit of America*" (7, author's emphasis). A black man named Wayne Williams was dubiously tried and found guilty of the last two murders (of two black *men*, not children) and by extension considered guilty of mass murder—the murder of the other victims who were all Black *children*— but Williams was not tried for the other murders. Circumstantial evidence and a "pattern" implied he was a mass murderer. Baldwin wrote "a man who murdered children was not likely to perceive a male adult as a male child" (5).

Justice Framework for Reading Eph 2:11–22: An Africana Womanist Perspective

As an African American citizen of the United States of America, I bear witness to the ways that the citizenship status and rights of African Americans and other people of color have been challenged, rolled back, ignored, diminished or violated by our fellow citizens, the state and officers of the state, the justice system, and the US Supreme Court. In recent decades, assaults on rights and privileges of citizenship often occur when majority white citizens and their representatives feel that their dominance, privilege, and power are being eroded as nonwhite populations increase and nonwhite citizens are able to take advantage of the opportunities of their citizenship status, despite historical barriers and contemporary injustices and inequities. Through a revisionist history, many dominant white citizens view themselves as the original citizenry that built this country with their sweat, brawn, and brains, rather than as the descendants of a whitened people who perpetrated genocide against the indigenous native peoples of this land and as the architects of perpetual enslavement and systemic and structural racism against blackened Africans and Native peoples.

The US Constitution bore witness to and codified the dehumanization and exclusion of blackened Africans by the whitened citizenry. Article I, Section 2, of the US Constitution of 1787 declared that for purposes of representation in Congress, enslaved Black people counted as three-fifths of the number of white inhabitants of a state, limiting the representational power of states with large majority enslaved Black populations. Black people were considered three-fifths of a person for the purpose of estimating the number of congressmen each state would send to the House of Representatives. In 1865, the Thirteenth Amendment to the US Constitution ended enslavement, but not racial discrimination. In 1868, the Fourteenth Amendment granted citizenship and equal civil rights to African Americans and the formerly enslaved, but it too did not end racial violence and discrimination. Yet, in 1869, the first Black man was elected to the House of Representatives. Hiram Revels of Mississippi was the first Black man elected to the US Senate and was sworn in on February 25, 1870. Joseph Rainey of South Carolina was the first elected to the House of Representatives and was sworn in on December 12, 1870. The Fifteenth Amendment to the US Constitution, the third and final improvement of the reconstruction era, was ratified on February 3, 1870. It prohibited the federal government and each state from denying or abridging a citizen's right to vote on the basis of race, color or one's former social reality of enslavement. Black people witnessed the violent white backlash. Between 1882 and 1968, white mobs lynched 4743 citizens, most of whom were Black men and women executed in the Southern states of Mississippi, Georgia, and Texas.

At the turn of the century, entire black communities were destroyed and Black people were murdered by white mobs in cities such as Atlanta, Georgia (1906) and Tulsa, Oklahoma (1921). Many political gains that Black people achieved after the civil war during reconstruction were erased or diminished. Black people could not vote without facing violence. Citizenship never guarantees the absence of violence or the creation of equality or equity when the dominant view themselves as superior and entitled.

The passing of 1965 Voting Rights Act expanded the Fourteenth and Fifteenth Amendments prohibiting voter discrimination based on race. In 1966, Edward W. Brook III of Massachusetts became the first Republican US Senator since 1881; he served from 1967 to 1979, being re-elected to several terms. The next Republican Senator would be Tim Scott of South Carolina elected in 2013. The first African American Democrat elected to the US Senate was Carol Moseley Braun of Illinois (1993–97). Barack H. Obama would hold that seat from 2007–9. President Obama was, of course, the first African American elected to the office of President in 2009, but not without having his citizenship challenged during and after the election. In 2017, Kamala Harris would become Black person, man or woman, elected to the US Senate from California, and in 2021 the first Black woman Vice President of the United States. In 2021, Rev. Dr. Raphael Warnock was elected the first African American US Senator from Georgia. As a nation, we are still witnessing many firsts, including this year in 2022, when Judge Ketanji Brown Jackson was confirmed as the first African American woman appointed to the US Supreme Court, but not without violent attacks on her record and humanity. Republican senators asked questions like "Can you define what it means to be a woman?" and accused her of ruling in favor of pedophiles. Judge Jackson took her seat among a majority conservative US Supreme Court intent on reversing equal rights gains of the past, as demonstrated when it overturned *Roe v. Wade* (1973) in its 2022 decision of *Dobbs v. Jackson*. That case, decided before Justice Jackson took her seat on the Court, disproportionately impacts poor Black women, and their right to make their own reproductive choices. Justice Jackson will be a dissenting voice on the court. African American citizens continue to struggle for unencumbered access to the ballot, and equality and equity in all areas of life, as the majority conservative US Supreme Court rolls back voting and other rights.

Revisionist narratives of origins and claims to the only legitimate epistemologies are tools that the dominant deploy to control the terms upon which the marginalized are granted (or denied) citizenship, the rights of citizenship, and the protection of those rights. In a society that is built on a racialized foundation that views the racialized other as inferior to the racialized majority, the minoritized other will be forced into a perennial and traumatically violent struggle for equality and equity. In this chapter I propose to provide an outline and model for reading Eph 2:11–22 through an Africana hermeneutical framework that places an analysis of the biblical text in conversation with the Africana struggle for equality and equity.

Although the letter to the Ephesians inscribes Paul's name as the sender or letter writer (1:1; 3:1), it is most likely that a first-century CE disciple of the apostle Paul wrote it. I will, however, at times refer to the author as Paul. Based on theological, literary and lexical differences between Ephesians and the undisputedly Pauline letters (i.e., Galatians, 1 Thessalonians, 1–2 Corinthians, Philemon, Philippians, and Romans), Ephesians is considered a deutero-Pauline letter; its authenticity is questioned or rejected. (These differences do not mean that Ephesians is absolutely dissimilar from the undisputedly Pauline letters.) Ephesians is also considered a prison letter; Paul identifies himself as a prisoner in the letter and using the first-person singular pronoun "I" (3:1; 4:1). If, Paul, himself is a Roman citizen (as the Acts of the Apostles claims, e.g., 21:39), he hopes to enjoy the rights of citizenship granted him even as he is imprisoned and perhaps awaiting trial. Howard Thurman wrote in his book *Jesus and the Disinherited* that "if a Roman soldier pushed Jesus into a ditch, he could not appeal to Caesar; he would be just another Jew in the ditch, standing always beyond the reach of citizen security," but if Paul were shoved into a trench, he would be a Roman citizen in the ditch,[2] meaning that Paul would have rights and protections that Jesus did not have.

Initial Questions that Emerge from the Justice Framework

The following are some initial questions that arise from the justice framework:

2. Thurman, *Jesus and the Disinherited*, 23.

1. How do stereotypes and the demonization of a people through a revisionist narrative of history make it easier to disenfranchise and subordinate them as citizens with little resistance from their fellow citizens?

2. How important are rights and the protection of rights for every citizen and how has this been a struggle for African American men and women?

3. Can citizenship and the rights of citizenship ever be equal if peoples granted citizenship are considered inferior prior to the granting of citizenship? How do ideas of inferiority discourage white and nonwhite citizens from becoming collaborators with Black and Brown peoples in the struggle for equality and equity? What other barriers to collaboration can you think of?

4. How important is the historical relationship between racial-ethnic groups? How does history inform or impact present hostilities?

5. When or how is defining our identity as a people over against another people beneficial and when is it not helpful?

6. How can religion or theological constructs undermine or support equality and the granting and protection of citizenship rights to marginalized and racialized peoples? In what ways does public religious discourse undermine and/or support equality for African Americans and other minoritized groups?

7. How do patriarchal values inhibit the full participation and equality of Black women in church and in society? How are the two interconnected?

8. In what ways, how and/or why has the granting of citizenship rights for marginalized and oppressed communities, particularly for African Americans and Native peoples, not resulted in full equality and protection under the law?

Recommended Resources to Construct the Justice Framework

Brown-Nagin, Tomiko. *Civil Rights: Constance Baker Motley and the Struggle for Equality.* New York: Pantheon, 2022.

Brown-Nagin, Tomiko. *Courage to Dissent: Atlanta and the Long History of the Civil Rights Movement*. New York: Oxford University Press, 2011.

Crawford, Vicki L., and Lewis V. Baldwin. *Reclaiming the Great World House: The Global Vision of Martin Luther King, Jr.* Athens, GA: University of Georgia Press, 2019.

Hannah-Jones, Nikole, ed. *The 1619 Project: A New Origin Story*. New York: New World, 2021.

Kendi, Abram X. *Stamped from the Beginning: A Definitive History of Racist Ideas in America*. New York: Bold Type, 2017.

McGhee, Heather. *The Sum of Us: What Racism Costs Everyone and How We Can Prosper Together*. New York: One World, 2022.

Moore, Darnell L. *No Ashes in the Fire: Coming of Age Black and Free in America*. New York: Bold Type, 2018.

Zack, Naomi. *White Privilege and Black Rights: The Injustice of US Police Racial Profiling and Homicide*. Lanham, MD: Rowman & Littlefield, 2015.

Summary and Analysis of the Focus Passage and Emerging Questions

In Eph 2:11–22, the author directs the Ephesian gentile believers to remember their past when they were not believers or in Christ (vv. 11–12). Their previous life is defined in negative terms over against the circumcised Jewish believers: They were literally uncircumcised, in the flesh, which means the mature men, young men, and male children were ritually circumcised when they joined the Christ Jesus movement, if they were not already circumcised. They were without or estranged from the Messiah/Christ, which made them foreigners in relation to the citizenry or natives (πολιτείας) of Israel and aliens (ξένοι) of the covenant of the promise. Finally, they were described as living in the world without hope and without God (ἄθεοι). The following questions emerge for me:

1. How does one overcome all these physical, biological, cultural, nationalistic, nativistic, covenantal, spiritual, and theological barriers?

2. How does one come to terms with the idea that the virtue of one's previous existence, including one's cultural, lies only in remembering how godless and hopeless it was?

3. How are a people convinced that everything they once knew and experienced—the traditions of their ancestors, their culture, their rituals, their spirituality—was godless? What is the impact on them?

4. What convinces a people that their religion—their God, their Messiah, rituals, covenants—are the only legitimate ones and the only ones worth believing in and practicing and that all others are Godless and hopeless? What convinces a people that everyone outside of their world are living lives of hopelessness?

5. How does naming persons who practice a different religion (or the same religion differently) as aliens, foreigners, hopeless, and godless create hostility?

6. What is the impact of linking relationship with God to certain citizenship status?

Toni Morrison wrote this about foreignness and the identification of the foreigner:

> How do individuals resist or become complicit in the process of alienizing others' demonization—a process that can infect the foreigner's geographical sanctuary with the country's xenophobia? By welcoming immigrants or importing slaves into their midst for economic reasons and relegating their children to a modern version of the "undead." Or by reducing an entire native population, some with a history hundreds, even thousands of years long, into despised foreigners in their own country. Or by the privileged indifference of a government watching an almost biblical flood destroy a city because its citizens were surplus black or poor people without transportation, water, food, help and left to their own devices to swim, slog, or die in fetid water, attics, hospitals, jails, boulevards, and holding pens. Such are the consequences of persistent demonization; such is the harvest of shame.[3]

Consider that Israel, as the people of God, is not innocent and never has been (what people are?). For example, the prophet Hos 4:1–3 (NRSVue) has an indictment against Israel:

---

3. Morrison, *Source of Self-Regard*, 18.

¹Hear the word of the [YHWH], O people of Israel,
    for the Lord has an indictment against the inhabitants of the land.
There is no faithfulness or loyalty
    and no knowledge of God in the land.
²Swearing, lying, and murder,
    and stealing and adultery break out;
    bloodshed follows bloodshed.
³[No wonder]⁴ the land mourns,
    and all who live in it languish;

Yet, the author of Ephesians contrasts the former life of the gentile believ-ers—a past he does not want them to forget and they should remember in the way he has described it—with the present. Their *now* has been accom-plished through the Messiah/Christ's blood (v. 13). They have gone from far to near, so that Jews and gentiles are united in Jesus's Jewish flesh (v. 14). So have they become honorary Jewish men? The hostility that once divided them, because of the commandments and ordinances has been demolished, which allowed Jesus to create one new humanity consisting of Jewish and gentile believers (v. 15). The Greek word *peace* (εἰρήνη) appears four times in the passage and may imply the presence of physical strife among the gen-tile and Jewish believers in the Ephesian assembly (vv. 14, 15, 17). Not only were the gentiles formerly aliens (ξένοι), they were wanderers or homeless (πάροικοι) *but* through Christ they have been made citizens-united or co-citizens (συμπολῖται) with the holy ones and members of God's household (οἰκεῖοι τοῦ θεοῦ, v. 19). That household has been built upon the foundation of the apostles and the prophets and the cornerstone is Christ Jesus, and that household becomes a holy unified temple, a spiritual habitation for God (vv. 20–22). Ultimately, the household of God, the temple, is not a physical structure; it is a spiritual one so that its boundaries, its walls, roof, and foundation are hermeneutically and theologically determined.

Here Are More Observations and Questions to Consider:

1.   Paul's use of the second-person plural pronoun "you" indicates a dis-tance between himself and the Ephesian gentiles (vv. 11–13, 17–19).

---

4. The translation here of ʾa-kēn as *wonder* instead of the NRSVue's translation of *therefore*, comes from the NBE (New Bill Brown Edition), my Hebrew Bible/OT col-league at Columbia Theological Seminary, Dr. William Brown, who offered this transla-tion when we co-taught a DMin course in biblical perspectives of justice in July 2022.

2. Paul switches from the second-person plural pronoun "you" to inclusive pronouns (i.e., "us" and "our") when discussing the specific work of Christ at v. 14 (he is our peace and has eliminated the hostility between us) and v. 18 (through Jesus both of "us" have access to the Father through one Spirit).

3. It is clear that one group, the Ephesian gentile believers, should see themselves as aliens, immigrants and strangers, despite that Ephesus is considered diaspora space for Paul and other Jewish people.

4. What does it mean to be without Christ and what or who determines when one is without Christ or with Christ?

5. Identify the power dynamics you see in the text.

6. What are the "covenants of the promise" (v. 12)? And what is the promise?

7. Identify the binaries in the text and complexify them.

8. Employing intersectional analysis, discuss the intersection of gender, class, sexuality, ethnicity, citizenship, religion, and age in the passage.

9. What laws and commandments does the passage refer to?

10. What pre-existing structures must the Ephesian gentile believers navigate as they become a part of the household of God that might be oppressive?

11. What happens when a people join a religion that does not recognize the foundation texts, intermediaries, prophets, and epistemologies of their racial-ethnic ancestors?

12. How does such a transition from outsiders to alien insiders affect one's self-identity or cultural-identity?

13. What are the dynamics of moving into a house and household that is already built to the specifications of the occupants?

14. In what ways is the peace described romanticized?

15. Whose testimony is being described in these verses? Who is the witness(es)?

16. How is peace contextual and decontextualized in these verses?

Becoming a member of a household or a citizen of a country does not guarantee equality and equity for those who are described as godless, foreigners, aliens, or migrants with homes. In fact, just the opposite. Some of those who considered themselves as citizens by birth—in a revisionist narrative of history that erases the violence of land confiscation and genocide—may continue to be hostile toward citizens they consider inferior, godless, undeserving, and perpetual foreigners. As I consider the justice framework or lens, I raise these questions:

1. What are the implications of connecting God-lessness or Godliness with nationality?

2. What are the barriers to the creation, exercise, and protection of civil rights of African Americans and people of color, of women, and/or poor people in the US (and globally)?

3. What impact do constructions of God or constructed theologies have in determination of citizenship rights, belonging, and violence in US society? Where do we see this happening in our present public discourse?

4. What are the implications and impact on a people who must be grafted into the foundational documents even though they were forcefully removed from their homelands to help build the country of residence and on later generations born into that same diaspora space?

5. Who are rhetorically constructed as the strangers, aliens, and foreigners in our society?

6. How do African Americans, other people of color, and women maintain hope and resistance when their citizenship rights are being rolled back and/or are unprotected on the basis, it seems, of moral imperatives exercised by the majority members of the highest court in the land?

Interrogation of the Passage in its Literary Context

The immediate literary context of our passage consists of 2:1–10, which precedes it, and 3:1–6, which follows our text. What are some of the interpretative connections between Eph 2:11–22 and the immediate literary context? In our passage, the gentile believers are accused of being without God and without hope "in the world" in their previous existence (2:12). In verses 2:1–10 the author explains what is meant by the phrase "in the world." To be "in the world," is to be disobedient, to yield to the desires of the flesh, and to follow the ruler of this world. But when the Ephesians were in the flesh/world, God showed mercy, grace and great love through Christ Jesus. In Christ Jesus, the Ephesians have been granted salvation and a new way of life. *What other connections do you see between our pericope and the immediate context that precedes it?*

In the verses that follow our pericope, that is 3:1–6, Paul testifies that he is a prisoner of Christ Jesus. He is likely physically imprisoned (at a location unknown to us), but the addition of the possessive phrase "of Christ Jesus" perhaps spiritually and psychologically mitigates and subverts his imprisonment. As previously stated, Ephesians is one of the prison letters. Christ Jesus is Paul's spiritual warden, and he is imprisoned so that he can fulfill his commission to proclaim God's grace to the gentile Ephesian believers (3:2; cf. Acts 19:21–41). In Acts, Paul testifies to the Ephesian elders that he is "captive to the Spirit, [and on his] way to Jerusalem, not knowing what will happen to me there, except that the Holy Spirit testifies to me in every city that imprisonment and persecutions are waiting for me. But I do not count my life of any value to myself, if only I may finish my course and the ministry that I received from the Lord Jesus, to testify to the good news of God's grace" (20:22–24, NRSV). The Spirit testifies to Paul and Paul testifies to gentiles and Jews. Acts and Ephesians agree that the content of Paul's preaching among the Ephesians was the gospel of God's grace.

We also find mention of the "apostles and prophets" here at 3:5 and in our focus passage at 2:20. The mystery of God's grace has now been revealed to Paul exclusively, skipping previous generations of human beings, but is disclosed to God's holy prophets and apostles through the Spirit (3:5). *Is Paul testifying to a hermeneutical privilege that enables him to read the prophets and apostles differently? Does Paul see himself as one of the holy prophets and apostles?* The mystery is the gospel that, through God's grace, grants inheritance, membership, and participation in the same body and promise as the Jewish believers enjoy in Christ Jesus (3:6). *What other theological or literary connections do you observed between our focus passage and 3:1–6?*

The word "grace" is not mentioned in our pericope, but the immediate literary context makes clear the significance of God's grace for the new citizenship and kinship/familial status of the Ephesian believers who are in Christ. God's grace, announced through Paul, governs God's household or administration of (God's) household (τὴν οἰχονομίαν) (3:2); through God's grace gentiles enter the household. This is the author's testimony! Thus, the verses that follow our passage delineated Paul's part in facilitating the citizenship and household status of the Ephesian believers.

The Broader Literary Context

The salutation of the letter identifies Paul as an apostle of Christ Jesus, which is God's will (1:1). Throughout our pericope (2:11–22), Paul refers to Jesus as Christ Jesus and never as Jesus Christ. His focus is on the work of the exalted Jesus as God's Messiah on behalf of the believers. In general, when the author refers to Jesus as Lord/master, he transposes the words placing "Christ" second, as in the greeting: Grace and peace to you all from God, the father of us all, and the Lord Jesus Christ (1:2; cf. 1:3; exceptions 1:5, 3:11). Perhaps this pattern signifies and emphasizes the historical Jesus's role as (slave)master and patriarch of the household of God. God the Father is the one who accomplishes all through Christ; it is God's household into which the gentiles enter, and they are reconciled to God (2:16, 19, 22).

It is in the letter's blessing where the ideas of adoption and inheritance are introduced (1:3–14). The transition from strangers, aliens, hopeless people, and outsiders to citizens and members of God's household is accomplished through adoption (not explicitly mentioned in our pericope but the reader will recall it from the blessing); adoption permits inheritance.

In chapter 1, the promise and work of the Spirit is both implicit and explicit. The Ephesians have been granted every spiritual blessing (1:3); Paul prays that they receive the spirit of wisdom and revelation (1:16), which the Ephesian believers will need to accept what has been written in his letter to them. In our text, there is only one Spirit that grants access to God (2:18, 22). And it is God who possesses power and who activated that power in Christ when God resurrected and exalted Jesus (1:19–20; 3:7). The Ephesian gentiles have been called to hope (1:18), whereas in their former lives they had no hope (2:12). But they are called to only one hope (4:4).

Paul desires to unite the Ephesian believers, Jews and gentiles. As citizens and members of God's household, the Ephesians are also part of Christ's body, and this new insider status comes with gifts, making some of them apostles, prophets, evangelists, pastors, and teachers (4:11). Paul is likely not the only apostles that has preached to the Ephesians, but he sees himself as *the* apostle to the gentiles, which includes the Ephesians (cf. Gal 2:7; Acts 19:24—20:1, where the apostle Apollos preaches in Ephesus);

he is an apostle by the will of God (1:1). Each of the spiritual gifts implicitly require or demonstrate knowledge, revelation, teaching, authority, and maturity.

In the broader literary context, the letter is quite specific and descriptive about the Ephesians' former life with God and Christ Jesus; it is absolutely negative and demonizing. The author puts flesh and bones on what it means for the Ephesians to have been far from God, hopeless, and Godless: They lacked understanding (were ignorant), greedy, licentious, practiced impurity, corrupt, lustful, thieves, full of evil conversation, angry, and bitter (4:17—5:6). They lived in darkness (5:8–11). Here are a few more questions that arise:

1. What does this imply about the Jewish believers?

2. How does a negative portrayal of a people's character, behaviors, and lifestyle encourage shame and self-hatred?

3. How might the description of Ephesian gentile believers create stereotypes and fear among their fellow citizens in Ephesus?

4. How does the way that the Ephesian gentiles are characterized convince you as the reader that the Ephesians are godless and hopeless? What is it that does not encourage you to question Paul's portrayal of the Ephesian gentiles?

5. What other questions might you raise about Paul's characterization of the gentile believers?

The Ephesian gentile believers who were once estranged, alienated, and foreigners must not intermingle with those gentiles who do not belong to God's household (4:17). This prohibition likely includes biological family members and friends who have not joined the Christ Jesus group. The Ephesian gentiles must dissolve all social, cultural, and ethnic ties; they are admonished not to associate with other gentiles who are outside of God's household. But God's household is no different from the average patriarchal Greco-Roman household (5:21—6:9). The structure of the household is the same: The husband is the Lord/master of the house, and the wife, children, and enslaved are to obey him. He is to love his wife, but she is to respect him. God is the ultimate slave master (6:9). Respond to the following questions:

1. Why do you think husbands are not admonished to love *and* respect their wives?

2. Was respect only due to men/masters?

3. Was respect possible without love in this first-century CE context?

4. How does the household code reinforce the status quo among enslavers/masters who join the Christ Jesus movement?

5. What is the impact of the normalization and Christianization of hierarchical oppression in a sacred text on readers?

The only difference between the household structure in Ephesians and any other in the larger social context is the rhetoric or confession of Christ as the head of the assembly of believers and thus of the household of God. Paul, as the earthly household manager or the domesticator of the gospel, assumes the power and authority to decide how the Christ Jesus household should function, but, of course, it is based on his experience as a male in a patriarchal culture. Perhaps, we might see this as the domestication of Christ and the Christianization of the patriarchal household, two sides of the colonizer's coin.

Questions about the Historical Context and Resources

We encourage you to explore one or two of the following questions or raise your own to research:

1. What can we know about the gentile and/or Jewish Ephesian believers of the first century CE?

2. What would be useful to discover about first-century CE Ephesus that would help us understand the gentile believers to whom Paul writes?

3. What other knowledge gaps can the Acts of the Apostle possibly fill?

4. What local gods/goddesses were worshiped in first-century CE Ephesus and how might that information assist in understanding the religio-cultural context of the Ephesian gentile believers?

Dialogue with Commentaries and Secondary Resources

You know the drill. At this point, readers should locate commentaries, monographs and journal articles, and book chapters to place in dialogue with the analysis of the focus passage.

Select Recommended Commentaries, and Other Secondary Sources:

Bird, Jennifer G. "Ephesians." In *The Fortress Commentary on the Bible: The New Testament*, edited by Margaret Aymer et al., 527–42. Minneapolis: Fortress, 2014.

Charles, Ronald. *Paul and the Politics of Diaspora*. Minneapolis: Fortress, 2014.

Fiorenza, Elisabeth Schüssler. *Ephesians*. Wisdom Commentary Series. Collegeville, MN: Liturgical, 2017.

Hawthorne, Gerald F., et al. *The Dictionary of Paul and His Letters*. Downer's Grove, IL: InterVarsity, 1993.

Kim, Yung Suk. *How to Read Paul: A Brief Introduction to His Theology, Writings, and World*. Minneapolis: Fortress, 2021.

MacDonald, Margaret Y. *Colossians and Ephesians*. Sacra Pagina 17. Collegeville, MN: Liturgical, 2000.

Martin, Clarice J. "The *Haustafeln* (Household Codes) in African American Biblical Interpretation: 'Free Slaves' and 'Subordinate Women.'" In *Stony the Road We Trod: African American Biblical Interpretation*, edited by Cain Hope Felder, 206–31. Minneapolis: Fortress, 1991.

Nicholson, Suzanne. "Ephesians." In *Wesley One Volume Commentary*, edited by Kenneth J. Collins and Robert W. Wall, 783–94. Nashville: Abingdon, 2020.

Sechrest, Love Lazarus. *Race and Rhyme: Rereading the New Testament*. Grand Rapids, MI: Eerdmans, 2022.

Smith, Mitzi J. "Ephesians." In *True To Our Native Land. An African American Commentary of the New Testament*, edited by Brian Blount, 348–62. Minneapolis: Fortress, 2007.

9

John Testifies

Apocalypse **Now** *(Revelation 1:1–8)*

By Michael Newheart

WE NOW COME TO the revolting, revealing book of Revelation, also called the Apocalypse of John. The book reminds me of the time in my teenage years when I was a Hal Lindsey-ite for a New York minute. Surprising, isn't it? It's surprising to me. The church in which I grew up, Second Baptist Church (2BC) of Liberty, Missouri, functioned as a First Baptist county seat church, that is, it had several movers and shakers in the town and county. The world was just fine the way it was. Folks were not particularly looking for the end of the world. Also, 2BC was just a few blocks from the local Baptist college, William Jewell College, and the church had among its number several professors, including professors from the religion department.

Such a church does not seem to fit the profile of a church of Lindsey-ites, of Darbyite dispensationalists. But I was a young man on fire for Jesus, looking forward to the Second Coming, and so I turned to what any self-respecting Jesus-freak wannabe would turn to: *The Late Great Planet Earth*[1] and its accompanying mental gyrations, which took the Bible in one hand and the newspaper in the other to find out how the Bible had been fulfilled in the day's events. In some ways, it was like a scavenger hunt, reading the newspaper and then scouring the Bible to find a passage that was fulfilled by current events.

---

1. Lindsey, *Late Great Planet*.

Adolescence is an apocalyptic time, especially if your father is termi-nally ill, as mine was. My world was ending anyway; it might as well be with a big bang. I was uninterested in social issues, which my pastor often preached upon. I remember thinking about writing him a letter in which I suggested that he preach more about The Second Coming of Jesus, which I thought was imminent, rather than issues such as the Vietnam War and racial struggle.

I never wrote such a letter. I just delved more into Lindsey and his dispensationalism, with the "signs of the times" to discern to be ready for Christ's return. Prior to my father's death in 1971, the day after my sixteenth birthday, my dad Edward Efton Willett suffered from a variety of ailments kicked up by a severe case of diabetes. He was in and out of the hospital during my early high school years. This man who had been my rock turned quickly to quicksand.

Lindsey-ism brought some certainty into an ambiguous situation. What could be more uplifting than the assurance that Jesus is coming soon? And around the country, the "Jesus Revolution" was happening. Ex-hippies were turning to Jesus! It was time of great revival, it seemed, and I wanted in on it!

I was not a long-term Lindsey-ite, though. I did not have the church structure to feed me in this perspective. I think that I went from Hal Lind-sey and *The Late Great Planet Earth* to Ray Summers and *Worthy Is the Lamb*, a book by a Baylor University professor that located Revelation squarely in the first century. I remember serving Memorial Baptist Church in Columbus, Indiana, when I was in graduate school. Church members wanted me to teach a Bible study on Revelation. They were interested in more of a Lindsey-style study, but since I was in graduate school, I gave them a historical-critical study, using Summers's book. "This is what Rev-elation is about?!" one church member exclaimed. As a result, I think that he preferred the Sermon on the Mount to the Apocalypse of John.

With the pandemic, the January 6, 2021 hearings, unbearable heat in many places, the Ukrainian war, we are living in apocalyptic times, but what is being revealed? Perhaps the Apocalypse of John does have something to say to us. We will give attention to the opening passage of the book, 1:1–8:

> [1]An unveiling of Jesus Messiah,
> Which God gave to him to show to his enslaved people,
> What must happen shortly,
> And he communicated it by

Sending his messenger to his enslaved person John,
²Who testified to the word of God and to the testimony of Jesus Messiah,
What things he saw.
³Honored is the one who reads and the ones who hear the words of prophecy
And who obey the things written in it,
For the time is at hand.
⁴John to the seven assemblies that are in Asia;
Grace to you and peace from the one who is and was and is coming,
And from the seven spirits that are before his throne,
⁵And from Jesus Messiah,
The faithful witness,
The firstborn of the dead and the ruler of the kings of the earth.
To the one who loves us and loosed us
From our sins through his blood—
⁶And made us a kingdom,
priests to his God and Creator—
To him be glory and power forever and ever.
Amen.
⁷Witness: he comes with the clouds,
And every eye will see him,
Especially the ones who pierced him,
And all the tribes of the earth will mourn over him.
Yes, amen.
⁸I am the Alpha and the Omega,
says the Master, God,
Who is and was and is coming,
the All-powerful One.

Let us begin with some questions about this passage.

* What might an "unveiling" of Jesus Messiah mean? Is it an unveiling that belongs to Jesus or that concerns Jesus? What difference does it make?

* John testified to Jesus's testimony. What might that mean?

* Count the number of times a form of the word "testimony" or "testify" or "witness" appears in this passage. How are they similar? How are they different? What kind of witness or testimony is being presented in this passage?

* "His enslaved people" and "his enslaved person John" are translations of phrases that are often translated as "his servants" and "his servant

John." How do you respond to the translation "enslaved person/people"?

* What might it mean that "the time is at hand" (1:3)?

* Twice in this passage God or Jesus is described as the one "who is and was and is coming" (1:4, 8). What might that phrase mean?

The Literary Context of the Passage

This passage opens the book. It is followed by John's initial vision and commission (1:9–20), which is then followed by the message to the seven churches (2:1–3:22). The seven churches are first identified in 1:11. John identifies himself again and says that he was on the island of Patmos "because of the word of God and the testimony of Jesus" (1:9). It is usually understood that John was in exile on Patmos, but perhaps he simply found himself there during his prophetic activity. A loud voice tells him to write what he sees to the seven churches (1:10).

John then has a vision of the Human One. Much of this description comes from the book of Daniel (esp. Dan 7:9–10; 10:5–6). The Human One repeats what the loud voice has said, that is, for John to write what he has seen (Rev 1:19). John is a literate enslaved man.

And then we're off! John sees and writes about a dizzying series of visions containing angels (lots and lots and lots of angels), locusts, scorpions, lampstands, dragons, plagues, spirits, bowls, cities, and more. The key creature, however, is the Lamb, who emerges in chapter 5 as the one who can open the seals of the scroll, and in chapters 6 through 8, the Lamb opens the seals. The Lamb stands on Mount Zion along with the 144,000 (14:1) and provides a temple and light for the new Jerusalem (21:22–23).

"Testifying" or "testimony" or "witness" is prominent in the last book of the Bible, which is often called the Apocalypse of John, the Revelation to John, or simply Revelation. In the first five verses, the "testify" word group appears three times: John testifies to the word of God and to the testimony of Jesus (Rev 1:2), and Jesus is the faithful witness (1:5). And as we read the book, the witnesses are the "martyrs," those who shed their blood as their (or as a consequence of) witness to the faith (17:6; see also 11:3–7; 20:4). John is a witness, Jesus is *the* witness, and those who die for their faith are also witnesses. Think about the following observations and respond to the questions:

* The initial phrase of the book is usually translated, "the revelation of Jesus Christ," or sometimes, "the apocalypse of Jesus Christ." How do you respond to the translation above, "an unveiling of Jesus Messiah"?

* Skim through the book of Revelation to get a fresh idea of the content of the book. From skimming through, what do you think is being unveiled? And in what sense does that unveiling belong to Jesus Messiah? In what sense is it Jesus Messiah?

* What are the repeating words in the above translation?

* John is a witness, a testifier. (Sometimes he's called "John the Revelator.") What is his testimony here?

* How are you like John? What "revelation" have you received of late? What was being veiled to you? What has been unveiled? How has it been veiled? How has it been unveiled?

* When did you have a revelation or an unveiling or a disclosure? (I am using all three of those words synonymously.)

* The word "unveiling" above translates the Greek word Ἀποκάλυψις, from which we get our word "apocalypse," which has appeared often in contemporary culture. What does that word mean to you?

Jean-Pierre Ruiz defines an apocalypse as "a literary form in which a vision from God, often under the guidance of an angel, communicates in symbolic language God's hidden plan for history. Apocalypses often include visions of the heavenly realm."[2]

* How do you respond to that definition?

* In what ways does it make sense to you?

* In what ways does it not make sense?

John is a witness because he "saw" (1:2b) these things. He had a vision. He hears, he sees, he writes. A loud voice said to him, "Write in a book what you see and send it to the seven assemblies" (1:11). The Greek noun ἐκκλησία usually translated "church," is translated here as "assembly," so that John speaks about the "seven assemblies" (1:4). How do you respond to that translation?

John is also a witness because he testified to two things: (1) the word of God, and (2) the testimony of Jesus (1:2a). The "word of God" could

2. Ruiz, "Introduction," 2205.

refer to Hebrew Scripture, especially as it is echoed in the book, or it could refer to the revelation itself. The "testimony of Jesus" could either refer to the testimony that is given by Jesus Messiah or that which is about Jesus, or both.[3] Which seems right to you?

John is the witness to the witness of Jesus. Jesus gives witness to God; John gives witness to Jesus. Ruiz writes, "The chain of transmission comes from God through Jesus Christ, as communicated to John by an angel."[4]

* I use the term "messenger" for the term that is often translated "angel." Skim through the book again. Notice all the places where "angel" or "angels" appears in the book of Revelation. (There are a lot!) Exactly what is the angel or messenger doing?

* What message are they communicating?

* How are they communicating it?

Various folks are named John in the New Testament. They include John the Baptist, John the son of Zebedee, authors of the Gospel, Epistles, and Revelation. Although the case looks simple, it is quite complicated. Biblical scholars debate about it endlessly. John the Baptist (or baptizer, Mark 1:4) is his own person, but traditionally, John the son of Zebedee, one of the twelve, is said to be the author of the Gospel of John, the Epistles of John, and the Revelation to John. He led a full, long life, according to this traditional view. The most popular view among contemporary biblical scholars is that these are four different figures: John the son of Zebedee, one of the twelve, is different from the author of the Gospel of John, who is different from the author of the Epistles of John, who is different from the author of the book of Revelation. The author of the Gospel of John may have been a member of the same community as the author of the Epistles of John, as these four books share much of the same vocabulary and theology. Biblical scholars often refer to these books as "Johannine literature." A completely different vocabulary and theology is found in the Revelation to John. Even though the book is the only one that claims in the text to be written by John, biblical scholars generally do not include it in Johannine literature.

John says, like Paul and other letter writers, "Grace to you and peace" (Rev 1:4b). Grace and peace. That may be a strange way to begin this book that seems at times so ungracious and warlike (see esp. 12:7; 19:11–21). We

3. Ruiz, "Introduction," 2205.
4. Ruiz, "Introduction," 2205.

have intended to write this book with grace and peace. We pray that you read this book (and Rev) with grace and peace.

* To what extent does the book of Revelation exhibit grace and peace? To what extent does it not? What might it mean to read our book and the book of Revelation with grace and peace?

* To understand verse 7, read Dan 7:13 and Zech 12:10–12. How do these verses help you with verse 7? What questions remain?

* What associations do you have with clouds? What might it mean to say that Jesus "comes with the clouds"?

* What correspondences do you see between Dan 7:13–14 and Rev 1:1–8?

The Lord God says, "I am the Alpha and the Omega" (1:8). These are the first and last letters of the Greek alphabet. Read Rev 21:6. What might it mean that this statement is at the beginning and the end of the book?

Read the seven beatitudes of Revelation at 14:13; 16:15; 19:9; 20:6; 22:7, 14. What does John say about who is blessed? What does John imply about those who are not blessed and therefore are cursed?

"All-powerful One" is a translation of the word παντοκράτωρ, which is translated in the NRSV as "Almighty." I think of the hymn "Praise to the Lord the Almighty the King of Creation."

* How do you respond to that name for God, "Almighty"? The term appears nine times in Revelation: here in 1:8; 4:8; 11:17; 15:3; 16:7, 14; 19:6, 15; 21:22. Look up all of these verses. What do they say about the character of God?

* How do you respond to the translation above, "All-powerful One." Does that make a difference?

* To what extent do you think of God as All-powerful? As Almighty?

Martin Luther King Jr. concludes his famous "I Have a Dream" speech with these famous words:

> When we let freedom ring, when we let it ring from every village and every hamlet, from every state and every city, we will be able to speed up that day when all of God's children, Black men and white men, Jews and Gentiles, Protestants and Catholics, will be

able to join hands and sing in the words of the old Negro spiritual: Free at last. Free at last. Thank God almighty, we are free at last.[5]

* What do you think that King meant by using this "Negro spiritual" at the end of his speech, as he did often?

* What does the spiritual mean by Almighty? What does King testify by using the word Almighty? How was King testifying? How was "the old Negro spiritual" testifying?

* How is John testifying by using that word "Almighty," or "All-powerful One"? How is John testifying in the context of 1:8? How is he testifying in the context of the entire book?

In Rev 4:8, four six-winged, eye-filled creatures gather around God's throne and sing,

> Holy, holy, holy,
> The Lord God the Almighty.

These lines have produced a hymn that was hymn #1 in the *Baptist Hymnal* of 1956 out of which I sang as I grew up at 2BC in Liberty. "Holy, Holy, Holy." I did not feel very holy at all. And I certainly did not feel almighty. During my teenage years, my dad was dying. Yet I sang about "Lord God Almighty." I testified that God was still in control. Did I realize that at the time? No, I was glad that he was dying. Die, evil man, die! But I felt guilty thinking that. He was harsh with me. My mother once said, "He wanted you to be perfect." That reminds me of that key verse in the Sermon on the Mount, which concludes the antitheses (Matt 5:21–48): "Be ye therefore perfect, even as your Father which is in heaven is perfect" (6:48 KJV).

My father on earth sure wasn't perfect. He was aloof and angry. In some ways, I thought that his illness was a punishment for his failure as a father. But then his illness made him even more pathetic as a father. I remember one time he was angry with me and wanted to whip me with a belt. He was so weak, though, that I easily grabbed the belt. He told me to let go of it. I said, "No! If I do, you will hit me with it!" Our fight ended when my mother intervened.

I prayed that my father would die. And God granted my request: On October 13, 1971, at 12:02 am (two minutes after my sixteenth birthday), my father died. I felt guilty. Had I killed him with my prayers? My father

5. From Martin Luther King Jr.'s "I Have a Dream" speech (1963).

was not a Christian. He had been raised in a Church of Christ (non-instrumental) in Arkansas, but he did not affiliate with any church in his adulthood. One of his brothers said that the family thought of him as "the angry one." What was he angry about? I don't know. My father served as a rear gunner on a B-29, flying bombing missions over Germany during World War II. Was there something about the war that fundamentally changed my dad? (It's interesting that I wrote "dad" rather than "father." Do I feel more connected to him when I consider that war might have changed him? Provocative question.)

Indeed, according to my teenager theology, I thought that Dad was in hell. He had not accepted Jesus Christ as his Savior and Lord, so he was going to hell. And I had not witnessed to him. Did I bear some responsibility? I was angry with my father because he was not kinder, but I also felt guilty because I had prayed for his death, and I had not presented the gospel to him.

Only later did I realize that anger and guilt are simply stages of grief. Also, my progressive, moderate Southern Baptist church would not allow me to be fundamentalist, dispensationalist very long. My father, I believe, like all people eventually, passed into the arms of a loving God.

Is John the Revelator angry? Is he experiencing grief? I will answer that one for you: Yes. *Yes.* He is angry as hell at the Romans and their collaborators. Damn them all to hell, all to hell. Fry! Baby, fry. I remember that when I was teaching at Howard Divinity, I protested that this view of the end-times was monstrous. This is not the God of Jesus Christ. It's the god of Satan, and Satan is thrown into the lake of fire, and I'd like to cast the God of the Apocalypse of John there too. Fry, baby, fry! Well, maybe I didn't say all of that. But that's my own anger. My own. And that's *Ok.* Anger is *Ok.* *What is your view of hell, of eternal punishment?*

I remember that William Tecumseh Sherman said, "War is hell," and he ought to know because he certainly unleashed it on the people of the South during the Civil War. Existentialist philosopher Jean-Paul Sartre said, "Hell is other people."[6] All to hell with what these dead white men said. Perhaps we make our heaven or hell on earth.

* To what extent do you think so?

* What is heaven or hell to you?

* What do you think happens after we die?

6. The line comes near the end of his play *No Exit* (1944).

But I'm testifying. To what do I testify? I testify to grace. I read Revelation graciously. The tea bag I'm using today says, "Serve all in truth, in compassion, and in grace." I testify to all three of those, but right now grace is hitting me. Well, not hitting me, but loving me, and I'm loving it. Amen? Amen. How might one testify to grace by reading how John testifies to grace? Well, he testifies mainly to wrath. Why do you think that John testifies to grace here? How do I testify to grace? I testify to dealing with grace with people. Grace, as the hymn says, that is greater than all our sins. But I also testify to dealing with love with people.

* To what do you testify?
* How do you testify to it?

I testify to love. I read Revelation with compassion and grace.

* How does John testify to grace?
* What if I knew nothing about Revelation but 1:1-8?

That's interesting. John testifies about an apocalypse, an unveiling, a disclosure. Ooh! Do tell: What would be gracious, graceful? It would certainly be grace for John and his hearers to have an unveiling of Jesus Messiah. The one whom they worship and love. They are persecuted (1:9). John is on the island of Patmos. Perhaps it is because he was imprisoned there or exiled there, but maybe he is there because he wants to be.

It might be helpful for you to look at Patmos on a map. It is southwest of Ephesus in the Aegean Sea. Paul would have passed near it on his way to Rome, under Roman captivity, of course. John was on Patmos because of the word of God and the testimony of Jesus (1:9).

Just like John, I am waiting for the *Parousia*, the coming, the presence. I am expecting the end of history as I know it anytime soon. I write during the COVID-19 pandemic and the Ukrainian war. It is certainly a time of violence and suffering and death, but the end is not near. Nevertheless, I am waiting—for peace. It is in my grasp, in my grasp of grace. I see it but don't see it. I wait. I wait. I wait for the unveiling, which may be as simple as the budding of spring or the smile of a friend. I wait. I center myself in my waiting. I wait. As Lawrence Ferlinghetti writes in his classic Beat poem, "And I am perpetually waiting / a rebirth of wonder."[7]

7. Ferlinghetti, "I Am Waiting."

Select Recommended Resources

Blount, Brian K. "Revelation." In *True to Our Native Land: An African American New Testament Commentary*, edited by Brian K. Blount, 523–58. Minneapolis: Fortress, 2007.

Blount, Brian K. *Can I Get A Witness? Reading Revelation through African American Culture*. Louisville: Westminster John Knox, 2005.

Carey, Greg. *Faithful and True: A Study Guide to the Book of Revelation*. Cleveland: Pilgrim, 2022.

Frankfurter, David. "The Revelation to John." In *The Jewish Annotated New Testament*, edited by Amy-Jill Levine and Mark Zvi Brettler, 536–72. 2nd ed. New York: Oxford University Press, 2017.

Moore, Stephen. "Revelation." In *A Postcolonial Commentary on the New Testament Writings*, edited by Fernando F. Segovia and R. S. Sugirth-arajah, 436–54. Bible and Postcolonianism 13. London: T. & T. Clark, 2009.

Mounce, Robert H. *The Book of Revelation*. New International Commentary on the New Testament. Rev. ed. Grand Rapids: Eerdmans, 1997.

Pippin, Tina. "Revelation." In *Women's Bible Commentary*, edited by Carol Newsom et al., 627–32. Rev. ed. Louisville: Westminster John Knox, 2012.

Ruiz, Jean-Pierre. *Revelation in the Vernacular*. Disruptive Cartographers: Doing Theology Latinamente. Maryknoll, NY: Orbis, 2021.

"Apocalypse"

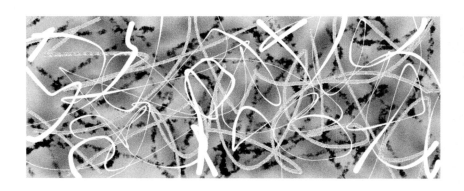

10

Epilogue

What Have You Done to My Bible?!

Newheart's Closing Testimony

WHEN STUDENTS COME TO seminary or divinity school, they often come with a rather naive biblical hermeneutic. It is "my Bible" and "my Jesus." They have a very personal relationship with their Bible and their Jesus, and that's a good thing. They often, though, do not reflect on the varied factors that have shaped their biblical hermeneutic and their Christology, whether those factors include their parents, their pastors, their Sunday school teachers, their church, their denomination, and the whole Christian tradition. These same students think that "my Bible" is self-interpreting; that is, "It means what it says, and it says what it means," and "God said it, I believe it, and that settles it." But when students take their first biblical studies course in college or seminary, they realize that things are a bit different. The Bible is not a book that fell out of heaven directly into their hands. It's a collection of documents that has evolved over a long period of time and has fallen into a lot of people's hands. Or better, a lot of people have put their hands on it over a long period of time. The Dean Emeritus at Howard University School of Divinity, Lawrence N. Jones—who hired me back in 1991—used to say that first-year students would often quote Mary Magdalene at Jesus's tomb, "They have taken away my Lord, and I do not know where they have laid him" (John 20:13 NRSV). I sometimes note that for Mary, it was the dead Jesus that had been taken away, so that she could see the living Christ, who was appointing her to go tell his disciples about his resurrection and ascension (see 20:16–18).

So, what have we done with "your" Bible? I hope that we have transformed it into "our Bible," that is, the Bible as a community product. The authors are communicating their testimony, and we bring our testimony to our reading and interpretation of their testimony. In other words, these documents are grounded in religious experience, and they are produced to enhance our religious experience. The religious experience of the biblical authors is shaped by their context, and the religious experience of biblical readers—that is, us—is shaped by our context.

So, what have we done to your Bible? I hope that we have thickened and broadened it. As we read it and as someone testified, "we are surrounded by so great a cloud of witnesses" (Heb 12:1 NRSV). Some of these witnesses are the subjects of the biblical documents, some are the authors, and some—like us—are the readers and interpreters. Yes, yes, yes. We are—excuse me, We R—all witnesses!

Smith's Closing Testimony

We have attempted to demonstrate that we can never over-emphasize the significance of the readers' contexts for interpreting sacred texts, particularly the NT and the contexts of readers' lives. The contexts of our faith journeys and their impact on how we interpret biblical texts are not linear, and they are complex. The ways in which we view and experience life, faith, the church, religion, God, interpretation, biblical or sacred texts, and the interrelationship among them have been challenged, affirmed, and/or transformed through the span of our lives. Our experiences impact how we relate to the biblical witness or how we understand and approach our readings of the biblical witness. The Spirit works with what we have and who we are at any point in our lives. The Spirit does not override the limitations of our humanity or human understanding. How we interpret and what we do with our interpretations matter greatly. Our interpretations inform how we relate to our neighbors, what we prioritize, how we live our individual lives, our treatment of Momma Earth, and so forth. Our constructed theologies are grounded in our (or others') interpretations of Scripture.

Testimonies can take the form of poetry, short stories, lament, letters, apocalyptic literature, gospels, biography, and memoir. As co-authors, our testimonies are, perhaps, a combination of autobiography and memoir. We don't (and can't here) share our entire life stories, but we do critically reflect upon pivotal episodes of our lives. Like memoir, our testimonies are a collection of memories. The memories we have chosen to share specifically relate to our contextual interpretations of Scripture and how our relationships to the biblical witnesses have evolved or changed through select experiences and through time. We invite our readers—college students, seminary and divinity school students, members of faith communities, and others—to reflect too—to consider and recollect your own interpretative journeys and how your experiences, communities, and institutions have impacted and continue to influence how you read the testimonies in the biblical witness.

Students too often attend seminary because they think it is a place where instructors will simply affirm what they think they already know about the Bible, biblical interpretation, and its relevancy for ministry in the church that is in the world. Thus, they see no need to read, re-read, rinse (read as if you never read the text before) and repeat. Some students, even those who are already pastors, assert that they cannot take what they have learned in seminary into the church! I ask, "why not, if church members look to you for guidance, trust you, and grant you authority to teach and preach?" This sharing includes teaching parishioners to raise their own questions and welcoming those questions.

The opposite can be true as well. Students sometimes arrived at seminary or divinity school in search of answers. In my first or second year of teaching, a student, who served as a senior pastor at a Detroit area Baptist church, stood up in my introductory OT/HB class of about fifty students and raised his hand to say, "We pay you to give us answers!" I responded, rather quickly, "I am not here to give you answers, but to help you think for yourself and to think critically!" I think the truth lies somewhere in the middle; it is more complex than either of us allowed. We are taught to memorize and learn/receive *the* answers in our homes, schools, and churches. We are told or given the impression that our teachers, scholars, and pastors have all or the most legitimate and right answers. After some thought, I realized that I could not expect students to know how to ask questions or feel confident asking questions when they've spent most of their lives surrendering their agency to other people considered more knowledgeable. I resisted being "pastoral" in the classroom, but changed my mind. I needed to model what I was teaching: the skills for asking questions and critical thinking and adopt what I coined (I think) *hermeneutical humility* (i.e., I don't have all the answers or questions, I don't need to act as if I do, your questions are as important as mine, and I can and sometimes must change my mind about my interpretations and constructed theologies.). In my experience, many students need practice asking or raising questions. I have had students tell me, in frustration, that they don't know where to start raising questions or what questions to ask.

Students also enroll in seminary, in my experience, for consolation, for safe space to lament, for healing, and to find justice. It was not uncommon when I taught at Ashland in Detroit, for Black female students to share in an "exegesis" paper that they had been raped or that one of their children had been murdered. In my first year of teaching I taught a biblical hermeneutics course in which a Black male student shared with me that his son had been killed and he was hoping to find answers or consolation. He chose to interpret a text from 1 Thessalonians. I recommended that he read Abraham Smith's book, *Comfort One Another: Reconstructing the Rhetoric and Audience of 1 Thessalonians*. The student later testified that he indeed found comfort in that book and in interpreting 1 Thessalonians. He subsequently left seminary and never returned, to my knowledge. Another student, a Black woman enrolled in my introductory NT course a few years later. It was obvious to me that she was distracted and it impacted her ability to do the course work. In a meeting with her in my office, she shared that her son had been murdered by her nephew (her sister's son) who had fled and evaded justice. It had been over seven years since he absconded and could not be found. Pastors with whom she sought counsel told her to leave everything to God and basically get over it. She no longer wanted their advice. But she needed justice. I told her that she was adding to her stress with all the requirements of seminary and perhaps she should take a break from seminary. I prayed that she receive the justice she needs. She took my advice and left seminary. About six months or so later, she left a message on my office phone to share that her nephew had been found and was brought to justice. She sounded like a new person. As far as I know, she never returned to seminary. The prevalence of injustice in our society and communities means that many suffer from the absence of justice. How shall we testify?

In my spring 2022 New Testament Interpretation course, I presented students with a draft of chapter 4 of this book as a model for writing interpretations papers that prioritize a contemporary justice framework. They could follow chapter 4 as a model wherein they listed critical questions at different stages in the paper (e.g., constructing the justice framework, analyzing the focus passage in its literary context, or discussing a relevant aspect of the socio-historical context of the pericope). Students that chose to follow the chapter 4 model did very well and raised excellent critical questions.

We hope that chapters 4–9 assist students in learning how to ask questions, in developing confidence in their ability to ask questions, and in the significance of their interpretations. Your questions and your voices matter. They are more than a gift, they are a necessity. Questions, and a diversity of questions from persons of various social locations, are often more important than answers. Some readers will not ask questions because they have been convinced that the only questions worth asking are those that can be answered. If readers want to explore something, don't know something, want to know something, or want to discover what it is we don't know, then start with questions. We do not need to answer all of or even most of our questions; some questions simply cannot be answered. Many of our answers are tentative. As of this writing, we do not know with any certainty who wrote the canonical Gospels. We can only hypothesize with *hermeneutical humility.*

Reading broadly and diversely will enable or compel us to raise different questions. The questions we ask guide our interpretations. And our interpretations will raise more questions. Our interpretations can motivate or compel us to speak or remain silent, to act or not act for good and justice, to comfort or further traumatize the oppressed, and to believe or not believe in equality and justice. Your questions matter and they are indispensable for doing creative and disruptive biblical interpretation!

A guiding question might be how can we hear and be guided by the God who is *Alpha and Omega,* who precedes the creation of the canon, transcends it, and continues to speak and intervene after the construction of an authoritative biblical canon? God is not the canon; the canon is not God. But the biblical witnesses, in their various contexts, testify—imperfectly and subjectively—about God, Jesus, and fallible human beings and institutions. The NT testifies that the HB Scriptures testify about Jesus through whom God brings salvation to the world (John 3:16). The language of testimony, the witnesses who testify, and the witnesses who see, receive, hear or write testimony are sometimes expressly identified in scripture, as we have shown. We are witnesses, as contemporary readers, to testimonies within testimonies inside of testimonies—a quadruple testimony tradition. In the Gospel of John, Jesus attended a festival of the Jewish people (his own people), and in his discourse to them, Jesus testified about testimony: "If I testify about myself, my testimony is not true. There is another who testifies on my behalf and I know that his [John the Baptist's] testimony to me is true. . . . But I have a testimony greater than John's . . . the very works that I am doing, testify on my behalf that the Father has sent me . . . You search the Scriptures because you think that in them you have eternal life; and it is they that testify on my behalf" (John 5:31–32, 36, 39, NRSV). God disrupts life and death to bring eternal life through Jesus. And yet, in the same biblical witness, Jesus testifies that his followers would accomplish more than he has done: "Very truly, I tell you, the one who believes in me will also do the works that I do and, in fact, will do greater works than these, because I am going to the Father" (14:12, NRSV). We have a powerful inheritance and responsibility to witness and embody that witness in the world. We are all witnesses. We have the power (individually and more so collectively) to disrupt injustice. How shall we testify?

The biblical witnesses repeatedly testify that God is a God of justice. Human beings who create poverty, can destroy it. Where we have a will, we will find a way. When are testimonies about God (and the Spirit or Jesus) in biblical texts oppositional or antithetical to justice (i.e., support genocide, the confiscation of a people's land, patriarchy, enslavement, and so on)? When do the biblical witnesses characterize God as a God of justice, wholeness/salvation, peace, steadfast love, mercy, kindness, and compassion for all human beings and creation? When are testimonies about God (and the Spirit or Jesus) in biblical texts at odds with the many witnesses in the same texts that command us to love God and love our neighbors as we love ourselves? What does God's justice and command to love our neighbors as we love ourselves look like in our contexts? Cynthia Moe-Lobeda argues that "neighbor-love as a biblical theological norm pertains to whomever one's life touches . . . [It] implies active commitment to the well-being of the neighbors . . . And finally, where people suffer under injustice, seeking their well-being entails seeking to undo that injustice . . . it is inherently justice-seeking."[1] It is the oppressed and violated (including Momma Earth) who have the most to lose when we do not prioritize (in)justice in the world and while reading the biblical witnesses. Where does the biblical witness value the humanity and well-being of all peoples and when does it not? When must we offer counter-testimony to a biblical witness?

1. Moe-Lobeda, "Love Your Neighbor as Yourself," 119–20.

We began this book in the prologue with a discussion about testimonies, primarily testimonies that are shared and heard in churches. You likely have similar and different experiences of hearing and sharing testimonies. You have testified, if not in church or in some other religious setting, perhaps to a parent, relative or friend.

This is a book of testimonies and about testimonies. Again, every testimony has context. The biblical texts as a collection of testimonies should be responsibly interpreted by reading them within their literary and historical contexts. But to privilege contemporary justice, the justice we need and that God calls us to create in our lives, communities, religious institutions, and in the world we occupy, we cannot simply *apply* our interpretations of the ancient testimonies to our own contexts. We have proposed starting the task of interpretation with contemporary justice issues or challenges and/or developing critical creative dialogue between ancient witnesses and contexts and contemporary witnesses and their contexts.

Our goal has been to provide pedagogical models for doing biblical interpretation that are creative and disruptive of injustice, and that demonstrate how we can raise many more and different questions in the process. Creativity, as well as learning, begins with raising different and new questions. In fact, difference is fundamental to creativity. In her essay "The Master's Tools Will Never Dismantle the Master's House" in *Sister Outsider*, Audre Lorde argues that difference has a creative purpose in our lives. Lorde writes that

> Difference must be not merely tolerated, but seen as a fund of necessary polarities between which our creativity can spark like a dialectic. Only then does the necessity of interdependence become unthreatening. Only within that interdependency of different strengths, acknowledged and equal, can the power to seek new ways of being in the world generate, as well as the courage and sustenance to act where there are no charters.[2]

Our cultural interpretations[3] are testimonies. Our silence in the face of injustice is a testimony. How shall we testify? Remember, we R all witnesses!

---

2. Lorde, *Sister Outsider*, 111.

3. See Felder, *Stony the Road We Trod*; Blount, *Cultural Interpretation*; Brown, *Blackening the Bible*; Wimbush, *African Americans and the Bible*.

Bibliography

Adayfi, Mansoor. *Don't Forget Us Here: Lost and Found at Guantanamo.* New York: Hachette, 2021.

Agosto, Efrain. "Philippians." In *A Postcolonial Commentary on the New Testament Writings,* edited by Fernando F. Segovia and R. S. Sugirtharajah, 281–93. Bible and Postcolonianism 13. London: T. & T. Clark, 2009.

Allen, Bob. "Mohler Won't Remove the Slaveholder Names from Seminary Buildings." https://baptistnews.com/article/mohler-won-t-remove-slaveholder-names-from-seminary-buildings/#.Y0WFEezMIq0.

Austin, C. A. J. *How to Do Things with Words.* New York: Oxford University Press, 1962.

AVP International. "Alternatives to Violence Project." https://avp.international/.

AVP-USA. "The Alternatives to Violence Project–USA." https://avpusa.org/.

Baldwin, James. *The Evidence of Things Not Seen.* New York: Owl, 1986.

Banks, Adelle M. "Report Ties Southern Seminary Founders to Slaveholding." https://religionnews.com/2018/12/12/southern-baptist-seminary-report-ties-founders-to-slaveholding-white-supremacy/.

Bazzana, Giovanni B. *Having the Spirit of Christ: Spirit Possession and Exorcism in the Early Christ Groups.* New Haven: Yale University Press, 2021.

Berger, Warren. *A More Beautiful Question: The Power of Inquiry to Speak Breakthrough Ideas.* New York: Bloomsbury, 2014.

Billman, Frank. "The Revival Roots of the Lay Witness Mission." https://goodnewsmag.org/2010/07/23/the-revival-roots-of-the-lay-witness-mission/.

Bird, Jennifer G. "Ephesians." In *The Fortress Commentary on the Bible: The New Testament,* edited by Margaret Aymer et al., 527–42. Minneapolis: Fortress, 2014.

———, *Permission Granted: Take the Bible Into Your Own Hands.* Louisville: Westminster John Knox, 2015.

Blount, Brian K. *Can I Get a Witness? Reading Revelation through African American Culture.* Louisville: Westminster John Knox, 2005.

———. "Revelation." In *True to Our Native Land: An African American New Testament Commentary,* edited by Brian K. Blount, 523–58. Minneapolis: Fortress, 2007.

———. *Cultural Interpretation: Reorienting New Testament Criticism.* 1995. Reprint, Eugene, OR: Wipf & Stock, 2004.

Bonhoeffer, Dietrich. *Letters and Papers from Prison.* Edited by Victoria Barnett. Minneapolis: Fortress, 2015.

Bovon, François. *Luke 2: A Commentary of the Gospel of Luke 9:51–19:27.* Hermeneia. Minneapolis: Fortress, 2013.

Brawley, Robert A. "Luke." In *Fortress Commentary on the Bible: The New Testament*, edited by Margaret Aymer et al., 217–63. Minneapolis: Fortress, 2014.

Bridgeman, Valerie. "Nahum." In *The Africana Bible: Reading Israel's Scriptures from Africa and the African Diaspora*, edited by Hugh R. Page Jr. et al., 194–96. Minneapolis: Fortress, 2009.

Brown, Michael. *Blackening the Bible: The Aims of African American Biblical Scholarship*. New York: Trinity, 2004.

Brown, Raymond E. *The Community of the Beloved Disciple*. Mahwah, NJ: Paulist, 1978.

———. *The Gospel according to John (I–XII)*. Anchor Bible 29. Garden City, NY: Doubleday, 1966.

Brown-Nagin, Tomiko. *Civil Rights: Constance Baker Motley and the Struggle for Equality*. New York: Pantheon, 2022.

———. *Courage to Dissent: Atlanta and the Long History of the Civil Rights Movement*. New York: Oxford University Press, 2011.

Brueggemann, Walter. *Living Countertestimony: Conversations with Walter Brueggemann*. Minneapolis: Fortress, 2012.

———. "Psalms and the Life of Faith: A Suggested Typology of Function." *The Psalms and the Life of Faith*, edited by Patrick D. Miller, 3–21. Minneapolis: Fortress, 1995.

———. *Theology of the Old Testament: Testimony, Dispute, Advocacy*. Minneapolis: Fortress, 2012.

Brueggemann, Walter, et al. *Struggling with Scripture*. Louisville: Westminster John Knox, 2002.

Butler, Octavia. *Parable of the Sower*. New York: Grand Central, 1993.

Byron, Gay L. *Symbolic Blackness and Ethnic Difference in Early Christian Literature*. London: Routledge, 2002.

Callahan, Allen Dwight. "John." In *True to Our Native Land: An African American New Testament Commentary*, edited by Brian K. Blount et al., 186–212. Minneapolis: Fortress, 2007.

———. *The Talking Book: African Americans and the Bible*. New Haven: Yale University Press, 2008.

Cannon, Katie Geneva. *Katie's Canon: Womanism and the Soul of the Black Community*. New York: Continuum, 1995.

Carey, Greg. *Faithful and True: A Study Guide to the Book of Revelation*. Cleveland: Pilgrim, 2022.

Chacon, Freddy. "Freddy Chacon del Real." *Facebook*. https://www.facebook.com/freddy.chacon.3760.

Charles, Ronald. *Paul and the Politics of Diaspora*. Minneapolis: Fortress, 2014.

Coady, C. A. J. *Testimony: A Philosophical Study*. New York: Oxford University Press, 2002.

Collins, Patricia Hill. *On Fighting Words With "Fighting Words."* Minneapolis: University of Minnesota Press, 1998.

Concannon, Cavan W. "Paul and Authorship." https://www.bibleodyssey.org/people/related-articles/paul-and-authorship/.

Cone, James H. *Said I Wasn't Gonna Tell Nobody*. Maryknoll, NY: Orbis, 2018.

Connecticut Friends School. "S-P-I-C-E-S: The Quaker Testimonies." https://www.friendsjournal.org/s-p-i-c-e-s-quaker-testimonies/.

Cook, Michael. "The Letter of Paul to the Philippians." In *The Jewish Annotated New Testament*, edited by Amy-Jill Levine and Mark Zvi Brettler, 354–62. New York: Oxford University Press, 2017.

Crawford, Vicki L., and Lewis V. Baldwin, eds. *Reclaiming the Great World House: The Global Vision of Martin Luther King, Jr.* Athens, GA: University of Georgia Press, 2019.

Crow, Joe. "The Cruciform Life: Michael Gorman on Paul's Narrative Christology." https://tabletalktheology.com/2015/09/24/the-cruciform-life-michael-gorman-on-pauls-narrative-spirituality/.

Crowder, Stephanie Buckhanon. "Gospel of Luke." In *True to Our Native Land: An African American Commentary of the New Testament*, edited by Brian Blount et al., 158–85. Minneapolis: Fortress, 2007.

Day, Keri. *Notes of a Native Daughter: Testifying in Theological Education.* Grand Rapids: Eerdmans, 2021.

E-News Now. "How to Testify in the Black Church." *YouTube*, May 20, 2016. https://www.youtube.com/watch?v=W2zgtG27H4s.

Fee, Gordon D. *Paul's Letter to the Philippians.* New International Commentary on the New Testament. Grand Rapids: Eerdmans, 1995.

Felder, Cain Hope, ed. *Stony the Road We Trod: African American Biblical Interpretation.* Minneapolis: Fortress, 1991.

Ferlinghetti, Lawrence. "I Am Waiting." https://www.poetryfoundation.org/poems/42869/i-am-waiting-56d22183d718a.

Fiorenza, Elisabeth Schüssler. *Ephesians.* Wisdom Commentary. Collegeville, MN: Liturgical, 2017.

Fountain, Matt. "Man Sentenced to Life in Prison as a Teen Is Released after 22 Years." *The Tribune*, April 30, 2015. https://www.sanluisobispo.com/news/local/article39527538.html.

Fox, Bethany McKinney, and John Swinton. *Disability and the Way of Jesus: Holistic Healing in the Gospels and the Church.* Downers Grove, IL: InterVarsity, 2019.

Frankfurter, David. "The Revelation to John." In *The Jewish Annotated New Testament*, edited by Amy-Jill Levine and Mark Zvi Brettler, 536–72. New York: Oxford University Press, 2017.

Freire, Paulo. *Pedagogy of the Oppressed.* Translated by Myra Bergman Ramos. New Revised 20th Anniversary Edition. New York: Continuum, 1993.

Friends Community School. "Mission and Values." https://www.friendscommunityschool.org/about/mission--values.

Gafney, Wilda C. *Daughters of Miriam: Women Prophets in Ancient Israel.* Minneapolis: Fortress, 2008.

Givens, Jarvis R. *Fugitive Pedagogy: Carter G. Woodson and the Art of Black Teaching.* Cambridge: Harvard University Press, 2021.

Gordley, Matthew E. *The New Testament Christological Hymns: Exploring Texts, Contexts, and Significance.* Westmont, IL: InterVarsity, 2018.

Gorman, Michael J. *Cruciformity: Paul's Narrative Spirituality of the Cross.* Grand Rapids: Eerdmans, 2001.

———. "Paul and the Cruciform Way of God in Christ." *Journal of Moral Theology* 2 (2013) 64–83.

Green, Joel B., et al., eds. *Dictionary of Jesus and the Gospels.* 2nd ed. Downers Grove, IL: InterVarsity, 2013.

Hancock, Ange-Marie. *The Politics of Disgust: The Public Identity of the Welfare Queen.* New York: New York University Press, 2004.

Hannah-Jones, Nikole, ed. *The 1619 Project: A New Origin Story*. New York: New World, 2021.

Hartog, François. "The Presence of the Witness." In *Testimony/Bearing Witness: Epistemology, Ethics, History and Culture*, edited by Sybille Krämer and Sigrid Weigel, 3–16. Lanham, MD: Rowman & Littlefield, 2017.

Harvey, A. E. *Jesus on Trial: A Study in the Fourth Gospel*. London: SPCK, 1976.

Hawthorne, Gerald F., et al. *The Dictionary of Paul and His Letters*. Downer's Grove, IL: InterVarsity, 1993.

Hobbs, Herschel H. *The Baptist Faith and Message*. Nashville: Sunday School Board of the Southern Baptist Convention, 1963.

Healing Communities USA. "Healing Communities USA." https://www.healing communitiesusa.com.

Historic Missourians.org. "Robert Sallee James." https://historicmissourians.shsmo.org/ robert-james.

Jackson, George. *Soledad Brother: The Prison Letters of George Jackson*. Chicago: Lawrence Hill, 1994.

James, Rob, and Gary Leazer. *Fundamentalist Takeover of the Southern Baptist Convention: A Brief History*. Santa Clarita, CA: Impact, 1999.

Jingsheng, Wei. *The Courage to Stand Alone: Letters from Prison and Other Writings*. New York: Viking Adult, 1997.

Käsemann, Ernst. "A Critical Analysis of Philippians 2:5–11." *Journal for Theology and the Church* 5 (1968) 45–88.

Kendi, Ibram X. *Stamped from the Beginning: A Definitive History of Racist Ideas in America*. New York: Bold Type, 2017.

Kim, Yung Suk. *Biblical Interpretation: Theory, Process and Criteria*. Eugene, OR: Pickwick Publications, 2013.

———. *How to Read Paul: A Brief Introduction to His Theology, Writings, and World*. Minneapolis: Fortress, 2021.

———. *Truth, Testimony, and Transformation: A New Reading of the "I Am" Sayings of Jesus in the Fourth Gospel*. Eugene, OR: Cascade Books, 2014.

King, Martin Luther, Jr. "Read Martin Luther King Jr's 'I Have a Dream' Speech in its Entirety." https://www.npr.org/2010/01/18/122701268/i-have-a-dream-speech-in-its-entirety.

Knapp, Robert. "How Magic and Miracles Spread Christianity." *Biblical Archaeology Review* 46 (2020) 50–53.

Krämer, Sybille. "Epistemic Dependence and Trust: On Witnessing in the Third-, Second- and First-Person Perspectives." In *Testimony/Bearing Witness: Epistemology, Ethics, History and Culture*, edited by Sybille Krämer and Sigred Weigel, 247–58. Lanham, MD: Rowman & Littlefield, 2017.

Kroll-Smith, J. Stephen. "The Testimony as Performance: The Relationship of an Expressive Event to the Belief System of a Holiness Sect." *Journal for the Scientific Study of Religion* 19 (1980) 16–25.

Levine, Amy-Jill, and Ben Witherington. *The Gospel of Luke*. New Cambridge Bible Commentary. Cambridge: Cambridge University Press, 2018.

Liew, Tat-Siong Benny. *What Is Asian American Biblical Hermeneutics? Reading the New Testament*. Honolulu: University of Hawai'i Press, 2008.

Lindsey, Hal. *The Late Great Planet Earth*. Nashville: Zondervan, 1971.

Lohmeyer, Ernst. *Kyrios Jesus: Eine Untersuchung zu Phil. 2,5–11*. Philosophish-Historische Klasse. Heidelberg: Winter, 1928.

Lorde, Audre. *Sister Outsider*. Freedom, CA: The Crossing, 1996.

MacDonald, Margaret Y. *Colossians and Ephesians*. Sacra Pagina 17. Collegeville, MN: Liturgical, 2000.

Mandela, Nelson. *Prison Letters*. New York: Liveright, 2019.

Martin, Clarice J. "The *Haustafeln* (Household Codes) in African American Biblical Interpretation: 'Free Slaves' and 'Subordinate Women.'" In *Stony the Road We Trod: African American Biblical Interpretation*, edited by Cain Hope Felder, 206–31. Minneapolis: Fortress, 1991.

Martin, Ralph P. *A Hymn of Christ: Philippians 2:5–11 in Recent Interpretation and in the Setting of Early Christian Worship*. Downers Grove, IL: InterVarsity, 1997.

Matthews, Shelly. *First Converts: Rich Pagan Women and the Rhetoric of Mission in Early Judaism and Christianity*. Stanford: Stanford University Press, 2001.

McFague, Sallie. "Earth Economy: A Spirituality of Limits." *Reflections: Yale Divinity School*, Spring 2010. https://reflections.yale.edu/article/money-and-morals-after-crash/earth-economy-spirituality-limits.

McGhee, Heather. *The Sum of Us: What Racism Costs Everyone and How We Can Prosper Together*. New York: One World, 2022.

Melcher, Sarah J., et al. *The Bible and Disability: A Commentary*. Waco, TX: Baylor University Press, 2017.

Moe-Lobeda, Cynthia. "'Love Your Neighbor as Yourself': A Call to Resist and Transform Economic Empire." In *Scripture and Resistance*, edited by Jione Havea, 119–34. Lanham, MD: Lexington, 2019.

Moore, Darnell L. *No Ashes in the Fire: Coming of Age Black and Free in America*. New York: Bold Type, 2018.

Moore, Stephen. "The Revelation to John." In *A Postcolonial Commentary on the New Testament Writings*, edited by Fernando F. Segovia and R. S. Sugirtharajah, 436–54. Bible and Postcolonianism 13. London: T. & T. Clark, 2009.

Morrison, Toni. *The Source of Self-Regard: Selected Essays, Speeches, and Meditations*. New York: Vintage, 2020.

Moss, Candida. *Divine Bodies: Resurrecting Perfection in the New Testament and Early Christianity*. New Haven: Yale University Press, 2019.

———. *Plagues of God: How Disease Shaped Religious Faith*. New York: HarperOne, 2021.

Mounce, Robert H. *The Book of Revelation*. The New International Commentary on the New Testament. Rev. ed. Grand Rapids: Eerdmans, 1997.

Newheart, Michael Willett. "A Hermeneutic of Human Dignity: The Future of Psychological Biblical Interpretation?" In *Psychological Hermeneutic for Biblical Themes and Texts: A Festschrift in Honor of Wayne G. Rollins*, edited by J. Harold Ellens, 121–39. New York: Continuum, 2012.

———. *"My Name Is Legion": The Story and Soul of the Gerasene Demoniac*. Interfaces. Collegeville, MN: Liturgical, 2004.

———. "Toward a Psycho-Literary Reading of the Fourth Gospel: What Is John?" In *What Is John*. Vol. 1: *Readers and Readings of the Fourth Gospel*, edited by Fernando F. Segovia, 43–58. Symposium Series 3. Atlanta: Scholars, 1996.

———. *Word and Soul: A Psychological, Literary, and Cultural Reading of the Fourth Gospel*. Collegeville, MN: Liturgical, 2001.

Neyrey, Jerome. *Christ Is Community: The Christologies of the New Testament.* Good News Studies 13. Collegeville, MN: Liturgical, 1985.

Nicholson, Suzanne. "Ephesians." In *Wesley One Volume Commentary*, edited by Kenneth J. Collins and Robert W. Wall, 783–94. Nashville: Abingdon, 2020.

Noah, Mickey. "Lay Renewal Weekends Lift Churche." https://www.baptistpress.com/resource-library/news/lay-renewal-weekends-lift-churches/.

O'Day, Gail R. "John." In *Women's Bible Commentary*, edited by Carol Newsom et al., 517–30. Rev. ed. Louisville: Westminster John Knox, 2012.

Omolade, Barbara. *The Rising Song of African American Women.* New York: Routledge, 1994.

Parker, Angela N. *If God Still Breathes, Why Can't I? Black Lives Matter and Biblical Authority.* Grand Rapids: Eerdmans, 2021.

Parsons, Michael. "Being Precedes Act: Indicative and Imperative in Paul's Writing." *Evangelical Quarterly* 88 (1988) 99–127.

Perry, Aaron. "Lift up the Lowly and Bring Down the Exalted: Gender Studies, Organizations, and the Ethiopian Eunuch." *Journal of Religious Leadership* 14 (2015) 46–66.

Pervo, Richard I. *Acts of the Apostles.* Hermeneia. Minneapolis: Fortress, 2009.

Pippin, Tina. "Revelation." In *Women's Bible Commentary*, edited by Carol Newsom et al., 627–32. Rev. ed. Louisville: Westminster John Knox, 2012.

Reid, Barbara, and Shelly Matthews. *Luke 10–24.* Wisdom Commentary Series. Collegeville, MN: Liturgical, 2021.

Reinhartz, Adele. "The Gospel of John." In *The Jewish Annotated New Testament*, edited by Amy-Jill Levine and Mark Zvi Brettler, 168–218. 2nd ed. New York: Oxford University Press, 2017.

Ridgeway, James, and Jean Casella. "America's 10 Worst Prisons: Pelican Bay." https://www.motherjones.com/politics/2013/05/10-worst-prisons-america-pelican-bay/.

Riggs, Marcia Y. *Can I Get a Witness? Prophetic Religious Voices of African American Women: An Anthology.* Maryknoll, NY: Orbis, 1997.

Rovner, Josh. "Juvenile Life without Parole: An Overview." https://www.sentencingproject.org/publications/juvenile-life-without-parole/#:~:text=Supreme%20Court%20Rulings,and%20applied%20othe%20decision%20retroactively.

Ruiz, Jean-Pierre. "Introduction and Annotations to the Book of Revelation." In *The New Oxford Annotated Bible: New Revised Standard Version*, edited by Michael Coogan, 2203–31. 5th ed. New York: Oxford University Press, 2018.

Sanders, James A. "First Testament and Second." *Biblical Theology Bulletin* 17 (2016) 47–49. https://journals.sagepub.com/doi/10.1177/014610798701700202.

Second Baptist Church, Suffield, Connecticut. "Mission Statement." https://www.secondbaptistsuffield.org/mission-statement.

Segovia, Fernando. "John." In *A Postcolonial Commentary on the New Testament Writings*, edited by Fernando F. Segovia and R. S. Sugirtharajah, 156–93. Bible and Postcolonianism 13. London: T. & T. Clark, 2009.

Segovia, Fernando, and Mary Ann Tolbert, eds. *Reading from This Place.* 2 vols. Minneapolis: Fortress, 1995.

Shakur, Tupac. "Keep Ya Head Up." *YouTube*, n.d. https://www.youtube.com/watch?v=XW.

Sharp, Carolyn J. *Wrestling the Word: The Hebrew Scriptures and the Christian Believer.* Louisville: Westminster John Knox, 2010.

Shiner, Whitney. *Proclaiming the Gospel: First-Century Performance of Mark.* Harrisburg, PA: Trinity, 2003.

Skinner, Matthew. *Intrusive God, Disruptive Gospel: Encountering the Divine in the Book of Acts.* Grand Rapids: Brazos, 2016.

Skitolsky, Lissa. *Hip-Hop as Philosophical Text and Testimony: Can I Get a Witness?* Lanham MD: Rowman & Littlefield, 2020.

Smiley, Joseph Bert. "St. Peter at the Gate." https://www.poetrynook.com/poem/st-peter-gate.

Smith, Abraham. "'A Second Step in African American Biblical Interpretation: A Generic Reading Analysis of Acts 8:26–40." *Reading from This Place: Social Location and Biblical Interpretation in the U.S.*, edited by Fernando F. Segovia and Mary Ann Tolbert, 1:13–30. Minneapolis: Fortress, 1998.

Smith, Mitzi J. "Abolitionist Messiah: A Man Named Jesus Born of a *Doulē.*" In *Bitter the Chastening Rod*, edited by Mitzi J. Smith et al., 53–70. Lanham, MD: Lexington/Fortress Academic, 2022.

————. "Ephesians." In *True To Our Native Land: An African American Commentary of the New Testament*, edited by Brian Blount, 348–62. Minneapolis: Fortress, 2007.

————. "Give Them What You Have": A Womanist Reading of the Matthean Feeding Miracle (Matt 14:13–21)." *Journal of Bible and Human Transformation* 3 (2013) 1–22.

————. "Hagar's Children Still *Ain't* Free: Paul's Counterterror Rhetoric, Constructed Identity, Enslavement, and Galatians 3:28." In *Minoritized Women Reading Race and Ethnicity: Intersectional Approaches to Constructed Identity and Early Christian Texts*, edited by Mitzi J. Smith and Jin Young Choi, 45–70. Lanham, MD: Rowman & Littlefield, 2020.

————. "'He Never Said a Mumbalin' Word': A Womanist Perspective of Crucifixion, Sexual Violence, and Sacralized Silence." In *When Did We See You Naked? Jesus as a Victim of Sexual Violence*, edited by Jayme Reaves et al., 46–66. London: SCM, 2021.

————. *Insights from African American Biblical Interpretation.* Insights 3. Minneapolis: Fortress, 2017.

————. "'Knowing More Than Is Good for One': A Womanist Interrogation of the Matthean Great Commission." In *I Found God in Me: A Womanist Biblical Interpretation Reader*, edited by Mitzi J. Smith, 236–65. Eugene, OR: Cascade, 2015.

————. *The Literary Construction of the Other in the Acts of the Apostles: Charismatic Others, The Jews, and Women.* Eugene, OR: Pickwick, 2011.

————. *Womanist Sass and Talk Back: Social (In)Justice, Intersectionality, and Biblical Interpretation.* Eugene, OR: Cascade 2018.

Smitherman, Geneva. *Talkin and Testifyin: The Language of Black America.* Detroit: Wayne State University Press, 1977.

————. "A Womanist Looks at the Million Man March." *Million Man March/Day of Absence,* edited by Haki R. Madhubuti and Maulana Karenga, 104–7. Chicago: Third World, 1996.

Solevag, Anna Rebecca. *Negotiating the Disabled Body: Representations of Disability in Early Christian Texts.* Atlanta: Society of Biblical Literature, 2018.

Stiles, T. J. *Jesse James: Last Rebel of the Civil War.* New York: Vintage, 2010.

Stokes, Ryan E. *The Satan: How God's Executioner Became the Enemy.* Grand Rapids: Eerdmans, 2019.

Stubbs, Monya. "Philippians." In *True to Our Native Land: An African American New Testament Commentary*, edited by Brian K. Blount et al., 363–79. Minneapolis: Fortress, 2007.

Summers, Ray. *Worthy Is the Lamb: An Interpretation of Revelation.* Nashville, TN: Broadman, 1951.

Sunnyside Baptist Church. "The Origins and Development of Baptist Thought and Practice." https://static1.squarespace.com/static/59488fec86e6c00d83cd97d8/t/595f bd79414fb508cbec7f18/1499446650022/Origins+of+Baptist+Thought.pdf.

Thomaskutty, Johnson, et al., eds. *An Asian Introduction to the New Testament.* Minneapolis: Fortress, 2022.

Tim. "Sartre: Hell Is Other People (Explanation)." https://www.the-philosophy.com/ sartre-hell-is-other-people.

Thurman, Howard. *Jesus and the Disinherited.* Boston: Beacon, 1996.

Walker, Alice. *In Search of Our Mothers' Gardens.* San Diego: Harcourt Brace, 1983.

Weems, Renita J. "'To Think Better Than We Have Been Trained': Thirty Years Later." In *Bitter the Chastening Rod,* edited by Mitzi J. Smith et al., 271–79. Lanham, MD: Lexington/Fortress Academic, 2022.

Willett, Michael E. *Wisdom Christology in the Fourth Gospel.* Distinguished Dissertations. San Francisco: Mellen University Press, 1992.

Wimbush, Vincent. *African Americans and the Bible: Sacred Texts and Social Structures.* New York: Continuum, 2001.

Wituska, Krystyna. *Inside a Gestapo Prison: The Letters of Krystyna Wituska, 1942–1944.* Edited by Irene Tomaszewski. Detroit: Wayne State University Press, 2006.

Works, Carla Swafford. "Philippians." In *Women's Bible Commentary,* edited by Carol Newsom et al., 581–84. Rev. ed. Louisville: Westminster John Knox, 2012.

Zack, Naomi. *White Privilege and Black Rights: The Injustice of US Police Racial Profiling and Homicide.* Lanham, MD: Rowman & Littlefield, 2015.

Zucchino, David. *Myth of the Welfare Queen.* New York: Touchstone, 1997.

Printed in Great Britain
by Amazon

19981631R10103